THE HAND
OF GOD

THE HAND OF GOD

OF GOD

*The Comfort of Having
a Sovereign God*

Frederick S. Leahy

THE BANNER OF TRUTH TRUST

THE BANNER OF TRUTH TRUST

3 Murrayfield Road, Edinburgh EH12 6EL, UK
P.O. Box 621, Carlisle, PA 17013, USA

*

© Mrs Margaret Leahy 2006

ISBN-10: 0 85151 944 X
ISBN-13: 978 0 85151 944 9

*

Typeset in 10.5/13.5 pt Sabon at
the Banner of Truth Trust
Printed in the USA by
Versa Press, Inc.,
East Peoria, IL

IN MEMORY OF
MY BROTHER GEORGE,
A BROTHER IN THE LORD

Contents

Foreword   ix

Introduction   xiii

Frederick S. Leahy, 1922–2006: A Brief Tribute   xv

1. THE HAND THAT CREATES   1

2. THE HAND THAT GOVERNS   20

3. THE HAND THAT PROVIDES   40

4. THE HAND THAT REDEEMS   61

5. THE HAND THAT KEEPS   83

6. THE HAND THAT GUIDES   104

7. THE HAND THAT CHASTENS   121

8. THE HAND THAT BLESSES   138

9. THE HAND THAT ENABLES   156

10. THE HAND THAT JUDGES   177

Epilogue: Comfort   197

Appendix A: The Historicity of the Genesis
            Account   199

Appendix B: The Baneful Influence of
            Evolutionary Theory   201

Appendix C: 'The Open View of God'   205

Foreword[1]

Anyone who has read Frederick S. Leahy's trilogy on the cross of Christ, *The Cross He Bore, The Victory of the Lamb,* and *Is it Nothing to You?,* as well as his study of demonology, *Satan Cast Out,*[2] will want to read this, his latest book, *The Hand of God: The Comfort of Having a Sovereign God.*

For many years Fred Leahy was the Principal of the Reformed Theological College in Belfast, all of whose teachers are also pastors in the Reformed Presbyterian Church of Ireland. This book mirrors his life; its pages display an extraordinary range of reading and a warm evangelistic tone. Here is an author whose first love has been to preach the gospel of his Saviour Jesus Christ, and this he has done faithfully for fifty years. Here are the mature reflections of an old Christian who has longed to pass on to those coming after him some insights from his life-long service of our Lord Jesus Christ. It is utterly safe and full of wisdom. To read it has been a means of grace to me; more than that, it has been a delight.

[1] This foreword was written before the death of Frederick Leahy in January 2006.

[2] All these titles are also published by the Banner of Truth Trust.

This book is a page-turner. Quotations and incidents from the lives of the greatest Christians, from the earliest Church Fathers to men and women of the twentieth century, fill its pages, giving a vividness to the narrative and constantly bringing one's affections to the truth. These examples show the ways in which the followers of the Lord Jesus Christ have endeavoured to serve their Master. No trial they have met from 'the hand of God' has been unique. Others have walked this testing way before us, and God has always provided a way of escape so that they could bear their trials with grace. 'You will be able to bear it too', affirms the author.

Let me summarize Mr Leahy's book for you. It begins with God, the Infinite Creator, the Almighty One, who made all things out of nothing by the word of his power, and all very good, the One before whose infinite vision we mortals float as specks.

This Living One governs all he has made, from the crashing power of the tsunami to the fall of the sparrow. He reigns over all his world, abundantly providing for all his people. By the incarnation of his Son, he visited and redeemed them from the power and penalty of their sins. He further preserves and governs all he has saved with a Father's love.

How wisely he guides them and how tenderly he chastens them to accomplish the goal of God-likeness in them all.

The blessings of his presence, his forgiveness, his service, and his fellowship, characterize all their happy days. He enables them to stand for him, and when they confront him on the day of judgment, even then they will lift up their heads as he acknowledges and welcomes them into their home. What comfort is theirs in the enjoyment and growing anticipation of eternal life.

That is what this book is about, but it also sets these truths in a framework of cosmic awareness, cultural tensions, ecological and moral concern, and a rich familiarity with how the world's greatest thinkers have responded to the challenge of behaving as believers in their own generation.

Church leaders often ask for books that make the great truths of Christianity accessible to contemporary people without triteness. They desire simplicity without banality, and respect for the immensities of the divine revelation of God without impenetrability. They look for an affection of tone without sentimentality and a directness without offence.

As you read these pages, judge for yourself whether Frederick S. Leahy has not succeeded quite brilliantly in this humble book, *The Hand of God: The Comfort of Having a Sovereign God.*

GEOFF THOMAS
Alfred Place Baptist Church
Aberystwyth
Wales

New Year's Eve 2005

Introduction

In the Bible we see God in action. The biblical focus is on God: God and creation, God and redemption, God and history, God and judgment. We also see God and election, God and regeneration, God and justification, God and sanctification, God and glorification (*Rom.* 8:29–30).

So what kind of a God is he? How do we know that he exists? What is unique about him? Can we know him? These and similar questions will be considered in the following pages. On what grounds can we look for the answers? We shall find them only because God has spoken to us.

Counterfeit gods are of necessity speechless: 'They have mouths, but do not speak' (*Psa.* 115:5). While we know little about the inner life of God before the creation of the universe, we do know there was a loving relationship within the Godhead: 'God is love' (*1 John* 4:8).

The silence of eternity was broken at creation: God no longer spoke within himself. The cosmic silence ended as God said repeatedly, 'Let there be . . .' Then he gave life to man, making him in his own image and speaking to him. God continues to speak to man; he does so through nature (*Psa.* 19:1–3), through history (*Isa.* 63:11–14), through conscience (*Prov.* 20:27), through his written Word (2 *Tim.* 3:16) and then supremely and directly in his Son (*Heb.* 1:2). God did not have to speak; to speak or to remain silent was his sovereign option. Always he acts as Sovereign, and it is this sovereignty of God that we shall now consider in detail.

Every worthwhile book should have an aim and should meet a need. In this book my aim is to show that the sovereignty of God, as revealed in Scripture, is a comforting truth. May this book help you, the reader, to see the relevance of this great Bible truth to the life of the Christian, and indeed, to the lives of all men and women everywhere.

I am indebted to Geoffrey Thomas for kindly providing the Foreword, to my sister-in-law, Eileen, who typed the manuscript, to my wife, Margaret, for her helpful interest in the work and to the editorial team of the Banner of Truth Trust for their encouragement and supervision.

FREDERICK S. LEAHY

Frederick S. Leahy, 1922–2006:
A Brief Tribute[1]

With a profound sense of loss we mourned the passing in January 2006 of the Rev. Prof. Frederick S. Leahy, author of the deservedly popular Banner titles, *The Cross He Bore, Satan Cast Out, The Victory of the Lamb*, and *Is It Nothing to You?* Professor Leahy died soon after posting his latest manuscript (the present work) to the Banner office. He was 83.

After he handed the package across the post-office counter, his wife Margaret, who was with him, suggested he might buy a new notebook to begin his next book. He paused before replying, 'Margaret, I think I've said all I want to say.' That evening he entered his eternal rest.

Born in Co. Donegal in 1922, Frederick Leahy prepared for the ministry at the Free Church College, Edinburgh, and Calvin Theological Seminary, Grand Rapids.

Ordained in Finaghy Evangelical Church in 1949, he joined the Reformed Presbyterian Church in 1953 and served three of its congregations till his retirement in

[1] This brief notice appeared in *The Banner of Truth* magazine for June 2006.

1988. In 1967 his gifts as a theological teacher were recognized by his denomination in his appointment to the chair of Systematic Theology, Apologetics and Christian Ethics in the Reformed Theological College, Belfast.

He also served as Principal of the College from 1993 to 2002. His books, into which he poured his love for the Lord and His gospel, and his skill as an evangelist and communicator, will endure.

We would like to express our deep sympathy with Mrs Margaret Leahy.

THE PUBLISHERS

I

THE HAND THAT CREATES

A lad who did well at school decided to pursue scientific studies. Before entering Cambridge University, he had come to believe that no scientist accepted the Genesis account of creation and that the evolutionary explanation of the origin of the universe was an established fact. At Cambridge he was contacted by the Christian Union and, accepting their invitation, was amazed to discover a sizeable group of science students who were keen Christians and who wholeheartedly accepted the creation account in the book of Genesis. In the providence of God, their witness was instrumental in his conversion. Doubtless the events of this true story have been replicated many times.

In view of that young man's experience, we may say that God wrote two books, the book of Nature and the Bible. Although the Bible is not written in scientific language, when properly understood, these two books do not contradict one another.

When we read in the Bible of God's 'hand', 'arm', or 'countenance', we are to think of God himself. As the *Westminster Confession of Faith* puts it, God is 'a most pure spirit, invisible, without body, parts, or passions'

(II:1). Nevertheless, God speaks to us in our own language in a manner we can understand – just as we speak as simply as possible when communicating with a young child. The Reformer John Calvin describes God's condescending to speak to us in these most striking words:

> God, having pitied my ignorance, brings himself down as much as possible to my capacity, so that he even lisps (as you might say) to tell me his secrets after a sweet and loving fashion, as if one wishing to feed a little babe should chew his meat for him, in order that he should have no more to do but to swallow it down . . .[1]

To begin with, God speaks to us about creation, a recurring theme throughout the Bible.

A SOVEREIGN ACTION

We are exhorted to praise the One who created sun, moon and stars, 'For he commanded and they were created' (*Psa.* 148:5). The heavens are said to be the work of his hands (*Psa.* 102:25). The earth and its inhabitants are to stand in awe of the LORD, 'For he spoke, and it came to be; he commanded and it stood firm' (*Psa.* 33:99). God declares, 'My hand laid the foundation of the earth, and my right hand spread out the heavens (*Isa.* 48:13). There was no universe until God 'commanded'. It was creation *ex nihilo*, out of nothing. God was the sole cause of creation. The whole of Scripture endorses the Genesis account of creation. That account leaves no room for

---

[1] John Calvin, *Sermons on the Epistle to the Ephesians* (Edinburgh: Banner of Truth, 1998), p. 423.

other gods, nor does the Decalogue. The first commandment quite literally reads, 'There shall not be to you other
gods upon my face.' The commandment demands that the
non-existence of other gods be recognized. The spiritually
minded Hebrew was well aware of the nothingness and
powerlessness of pagan deities.

It is equally clear from Scripture that God did not need
to create. Creation added nothing to God. As the *Westminster Confession* says, 'God hath all life, glory, goodness, blessedness, in and of Himself; and is alone in and
unto Himself all-sufficient, not standing in need of any
creatures which He hath made, nor deriving any glory
from them, but only manifesting his own glory . . .' (II:2).
How precise is the wording of that Confession!

However, God has willed to reveal himself, and to have
fellowship with others. This is the sovereign decision of a
God who is independent and self-sufficient. He is distinct
from his creation, as the Genesis account demonstrates,
yet not aloof from it, as the Deists taught, nor identical
with it, as the Pantheists imagine.

The God of Deism was an irrelevance for man in his
daily life; and the God of Pantheism being impersonal,
(the Pantheistic motto being 'All is God and God is all')
leaves the door open for what we now know as 'New
Age' philosophy. The first two chapters of Genesis strike
a perfect balance in this respect. It is important to see the
relationship that our sovereign God has to his creation in
order to repudiate the present tendency to worship the
physical forces of the universe and to combat the spurious
and idolatrous claims of astrology and naturalism. The

Genesis account of creation was never more relevant than today!

The crowning act of creation took place when God made man. Genesis 1:24 marks a new phase in the creation narrative: 'Then God said, "Let us make man in our image, after our likeness . . . then the LORD God formed[2] man of dust from the ground and breathed into his nostrils the breath of life, and the man became a living creature' (*Gen.* 2:7). John Murray directs our attention in these verses to the 'abrupt change' that takes place from 'after its kind' to 'in our image, after our likeness'. Here is a 'radical differentiation between the pattern to which other forms of life conform and the exemplar which is the model for man' . . . 'Man's origin is not only the unique subject of God's counsel; man is from the outset the recipient of unique endowment and dignity'.[3] Murray also reminds us that man's uniqueness in no way lessens his affinity with his non-animate environment (*i.e.* the ground on which he walks), and with animate creatures. Murray comments

> Genesis 2:7 . . . shows that man has affinity with the material stuff of the earth and with the animate creation as well. There is likeness and for that reason congruity. So we should expect resemblances of various kinds. If there were complete disparity, how incongruous would

---

[2] The word translated 'formed' (*yatsar*) means to 'mould'. It is the word used to describe the activity of the potter (*Jer.* 8:2 ff.) who attended to his task with particular care and attention.

[3] *Collected Writings of John Murray* (Edinburgh: Banner of Truth, 1977), vol. 2, pp. 4–5.

be man's habitat and vocation. We see the wisdom and goodness of the Creator in these likenesses. No evolutionary hypothesis is necessary to explain them; they are required by the relationships man sustains to his environment.[4]

Adam was the first man. Evolutionists refer confidently to Cro-Magnon and Neanderthal 'men', and some theologians are prepared to speak of 'pre-Adamic man'. What evidence is there that such man-like creatures possessed the mental, moral and spiritual endowments that Adam had? It is well known that some small creatures can use stones to break shells, bees can build the most complicated geometric hives, beavers can drop small trees in the right direction to build dams, birds and fish can migrate long distances and return unerringly. We need not be surprised, then, if animals, such as man-like apes, that stood upright, had even greater skills. But such creatures were not human as Adam was. The term 'pre-Adamic man' should have no place in the vocabulary of those who accept the Genesis account of creation.[5]

There is nothing in Genesis 1 to suggest the extensive geological time spans necessary to support the evolutionary hypothesis. Rather we see the evening and morning sequence of creation, and in it all we see the creative sovereignty of God. The framework theory, which has gained ground in recent years, conflicts with the concept of God creating sequentially day by day. This view sees the days of Genesis 1 as symbolic representations, somewhat like

[4] Op.cit., vol. 2, p. 13.
[5] See Appendix A.

the numbered visions in the book of Revelation. The theologian Carl F. H. Henry, writing about this theory, comments that the

> removal of temporal sequence from Genesis 1 seems to do less than full justice to the creation account . . . The Genesis account reveals an unmistakable creation-sequence count-down: 'First day . . . second day . . . third day . . . fourth day . . . fifth day . . . sixth day.' Is this chronological pattern of creative activity to be regarded simply as poetry? Or does it involve a validity claim that intersects modern scientific views?[6]

One wonders why some Reformed scholars adopt this view of the creation account, which removes the story of creation from its obvious historical framework.[7]

It is clear from Scripture that creation is the work of the Triune God. In a general sense it may be said that the Father commanded, the Spirit effected, and the Son sustains creation. In Genesis 1:2 the Spirit is represented as 'hovering over the face of the waters'. With reference to the inhabitants of this earth, Psalm 104:30 says, 'When you send forth your Spirit, they are created, and you renew the face of the ground.' The Son holds a unique place in the creation. 'All things were made through him (the better rendering here), and without him was not any thing made that was made' (*John* 1:3), not 'by' him, but 'through' him. As Leon Morris comments, 'This way of

---

[6] *God, Revelation and Authority,* vol. 6, p. 134.

[7] For a study of the creation and function of the angels, see my *Satan Cast Out* (Edinburgh: Banner of Truth, 1975).

putting it safeguards the truth that the Father is the source of all that is.'[8] 1 Corinthians 8:6 teaches us that 'there is one God, the Father, from whom are all things and for whom we exist, and one Lord Jesus Christ, through whom we exist'. The Father is seen as the author and Christ as the agent of creation. Colossians 1:17 affirms that Christ 'is before all things, and in him all things hold together'. He maintains the creation of which he was the agent. Without him it would not exist for a moment: not an atom or a cell can exist on its own. Creation is totally dependent on Christ for its existence, and as we shall see, for its renewal too.

We face a choice between the biblical doctrine of creation and evolutionary theory in our attempt to understand the universe. Some try to bridge the gap between these distinct positions by stating that God used the evolutionary process to bring about the creation of life in all its forms. Louis Berkhof calls this theory of 'theistic evolution' 'a child of embarrassment . . . neither the biblical doctrine of creation, nor a consistent theory of evolution', and 'a very dangerous hybrid'.[9] It is really a contradiction in terms.

The practical implications of the doctrine of creation are far reaching. Adam was given the task of caring for this earth. He was to 'work it and keep it', or 'till it and look after it'. His constructive task would be beneficial to

---

[8] Leon Morris, *The Gospel according to John* (London: Marshall, Morgan & Scott, 1971) p. 80.

[9] Louis Berkhof, *Systematic Theology* (London: Banner of Truth, 1958), pp 139, 162.

a planet that God saw as 'very good', a home in which man was to dwell (*Psa.* 115:16). But fallen man has exploited, defiled, and destroyed much of this earth. The extent of this environmental destruction is utterly appalling, and much of it is irreversible. Air, water, and land have been polluted. There has been a mass extinction of creatures and plants.

It is sad to think that some undiscovered species may well have been destroyed. Rain forests have been cut down in the interests of commerce regardless of the consequences for mankind and his environment. It has been asserted that the extinction of one species has a knock-on effect on at least sixteen others. Towards the end of last century it was estimated that 27,000 species were being lost each year. That is now seen as a conservative estimate. It must be remembered that extinction is absolute and final: it cannot be remedied in this present age. Man has abdicated his stewardship of caring for this earth. So where is the voice of the Christian church? How sensitive is the average Christian to this reckless mishandling of the earth? Why should it be left to 'green' parties, 'Friends of the Earth' and 'New Agers' to protest at man's plundering of the earth with insatiable greed, and to endeavour to conserve what they see as 'mother earth'?

This is God's earth, and man is not free to pillage and contaminate it to his heart's content. It is true that this earth is under a curse because of man's sin (*Gen.* 3:17) and that now we see 'thorns and thistles', a 'groaning', convulsed earth (*Rom.* 8:22), a hostile environment, bacteria, viruses and such like. However, all this does not mean that God no longer cares for his earth, or that man has been relieved of his stewardship. After the Flood, God made a covenant with Noah promising that never again would there be 'a flood to destroy the earth' (*Gen.* 9:11). That covenant included 'every living creature . . . the birds, the livestock, and every beast of the earth . . . as many as came out of the ark; it is for every beast of the earth' (verse 10). Clearly God still cares for this earth and the life that is on it. The Hebrews were taught to respect nature. The land was to have its Sabbath (rest) at regular intervals (*Lev.* 25:2, 4, 6). God said to Israel, 'The land shall not be sold in perpetuity; for the land is mine' (*Lev.* 25:23). Beasts of burden were to be used with consideration (*Deut.* 22:10; 25:4). Even the treatment of a nesting bird was covered by the law (*Deut.* 22:6–7). Then there is Psalm 104, a glorious piece of inspired song, which recalls the history of creation and shows God's bountiful provision for all his creatures.

Clearly man is accountable to God for the manner in which he treats this earth and its multiform life. God's wrath must be great as he views the current pollution of his earth. Yet it needs to be remembered that although man's stewardship is still binding, the Bible's focus is not conservation but transformation – a glorious transformation that will take place at Christ's return. Even the 'groaning' earth of which Paul speaks is represented as being 'in the pains of childbirth' (*Rom.* 8:22). There is hope in such pangs. As we shall see, Satan's persistent attempt to destroy God's creation has been rendered abortive by the cross of Christ.

Another practical implication of the doctrine of creation concerns the human body, designed and made by God, and undoubtedly one of the greatest wonders of creation. Scripture teaches that men and women are not free to do whatever they wish with their bodies, whether it be the wilful abortion of an unborn child or indulgence in pornography. The former has led to the slaughter of more human beings than perished in the Holocaust; the latter is a sickening rot at the heart of society. When the awareness fades that we owe our existence to God, respect for the human body diminishes. And yet in the Bible we see that the human body is God's handiwork:

> For you formed my inward parts. You knitted me together in my mother's womb. I praise you, for I am fearfully and wonderfully made. . . . My frame was not hidden from you when I was made in secret, intricately woven in the depths of the earth. Your eyes saw my unformed substance (*Psa.* 139:13–16).

Christ, the eternal Word, became incarnate: he became flesh, our flesh and our blood, and in that body he suffered to redeem us: in that very same body he was glorified and now he reigns in glory. It is a terrible sacrilege when the human body, designed and redeemed to bear the image of God in Christ, is degraded in pornography. It also cheapens and degrades sexuality and love. In western countries particularly, pornography is pervasive. One finds it in magazines, newspapers, and on the internet. Advertising is often steeped in it and young people are bombarded with the message that to be normal, attractive, and accepted by others one has to be sexually provocative. The pressure to conform to this life-style is great and the consequences are tragic. How often do we hear it said, 'I have the right to do what I want with my own body.' Nothing could be further from the truth. Before the law of God no man or woman is free to do with his or her body whatever they please. Though he may change the way he executes his judgments, the God who rained down judgment on Sodom and Gomorrah for their sexual perversions remains for ever the same and cannot change.

A REVEALING ACTION

In creation the glory, power, and goodness of God are revealed. 'The heavens declare the glory of God, and the sky above proclaims his handiwork' (*Psa*.19:1). Commenting on this verse, Calvin writes:

> When we behold the heavens, we cannot but be elevated, by the contemplation of them, to Him who is their Creator; and the beautiful arrangement and wonderful variety which distinguish the courses and stations of the heavenly bodies, together with the beauty and splendour which are manifest in them, cannot but furnish us with an evident proof of his providence. Scripture, indeed, makes known to us the time and manner of creation; but the heavens themselves . . . proclaim, and distinctly enough, that they have been fashioned by his hands: and this of itself abundantly suffices to bear testimony to men of his glory. As soon as we acknowledge God to be

the supreme Architect, who has erected the beauteous fabric of the Universe, our minds must necessarily be ravished with wonder at his infinite goodness, wisdom and power.[10]

Sadly, fallen man refuses to acknowledge God's general revelation of himself in creation. The Bible's doctrine of creation is largely discounted, even despised, in colleges and universities worldwide. Some people will not be happy until all reference to creation in academic circles is banned. The state-school curriculum has no place for the God of the Bible, except in terms of comparative religion, in which case he is reduced to one concept of deity among many. Yet man cannot alter the fact that he bears the image of God and because of that he differs radically from the beasts of the field.

In this determined rejection of the doctrine of creation, and almost fanatical promotion of the theory of evolution as a scientific fact (which it is not), we see fallen man's wilful suppression of the truth. This stifling of the truth is described in Romans 1:18–20: 'For the wrath of God is revealed from heaven against all ungodliness and unrighteousness of men, who by their unrighteousness suppress (not 'hold' as in KJV) the truth. For what can be known about God is plain to them, because God has shown it to them . . . So they are without excuse.'[11]

---

[10] *Commentary on the Book of Psalms* (Grand Rapids: Wm. B. Eerdmans, 1963), vol. 1, p. 309.

[11] John Murray prefers the term 'restrain' to 'suppress' in Romans 1:18, the idea in the original being that of 'holding back'. *The Epistle of Paul to the Romans* (London: Marshall, Morgan & Scott, 1960), vol. 1, p. 37.

Carl F. H. Henry rightly affirms that

> . . . the Creator God's testimony to himself in creation continues daily and hourly and moment by moment. Fallen man in his day-to-day life is never completely detached or isolated from the revelation of God. His frustrating of divine revelation is attested in part by the fact of human guilt, which presupposes revolt against the light of revelation. For this revolt against God's disclosure he is held responsible and not without guilt (*Eph.* 4:18). His revolt is attested also by the moral struggle that characterizes human existence (*Rom.* 2:15). Man's predicament in his estrangement from God is therefore not that of an absence of light; forever and always he stands in continuing relationship to the Logos [the Word] whose brilliance he constantly bedims but cannot extinguish. Never and nowhere are the heathen or any of us left without a witness to the living God, however much man deflects and ignores this revelation.[12]

The key word in that statement is 'revolt'. Against all light and evidence, fallen man closes his eyes, rejects the Bible's account of how things began and clings tenaciously to the theory of evolution. What a complicated and tortuous theory that is, as it speculates in terms of millions of years! By contrast, we are struck by the simple grandeur of the explanation that God has given us. Man's knowledge of the universe has made astounding progress in recent decades, and it continues to grow, but his understanding remains radically deficient in the critical points.

[12] Op. cit., vol. 2, p. 85.

There is a strange inconsistency in the mindset that declares one moment that there is no mind behind, or purpose in, the universe and that it is merely the result of blind chance, and the next moment speaks of the 'laws' of the universe! What is the origin of those laws? Why do they never change or fail? There is no satisfying explanation apart from God the Creator. There is, however, an explanation for man's refusal to acknowledge his Divine Maker.

Men are said to be 'darkened in their understanding, alienated from the life of God because of the ignorance that is in them, due to their hardness of heart' (*Eph.* 4:18). By contrast the Ephesian Christians are said to be 'enlightened'.

> 'Darkened' is a perfect participle, conveying the force of permanence. The apostle is not referring to an occasional dark passage. The mind without God (who made the mind) is permanently in darkness . . . Paul is still dealing with the mental processes of those who live without God. He is contemptuous of the attempt to make sense of life while leaving God out of account.[13]

There is much peace to be found in accepting the biblical revelation concerning the universe and life, rather than groping endlessly in the speculative mists of godlessness. There is abundant peace in recognizing the all-pervasive presence of God in his creation. A. A. Hodge states this reality so well:

[13] Leon Morris, *Expository Reflections on the Letter to the Ephesians* (Grand Rapids: Baker Books, 1994), p. 135f.

Every hair of our head is numbered, and not one sparrow falls to the ground except as our Father wills it. He
works in us all to will and to do his good pleasure in all
things. Hence every flower is a thought of God. The fir-
mament reflects his immensity, and the order of the stars
his limitless intelligence, and the myriad-fold beauty of
the world unveils the secret chambers of his imagery.
The tempest is the letting loose of his strength, and the
thunder utters his voice. To the Christian the universe is
not merely a temple in which God is worshipped, but it
is also the ever-venerated countenance on which the
affections of our Lord toward his children are visibly
expressed. Everywhere we see God.[14]

'Every flower is a thought of God', and every tree, and
every . . . but where shall we finish once we embark down
this avenues of thought? So Joyce Kilmer wrote

> Poems are made by fools like me,
> But only God can make a tree.

Well has it been said that the believing scientist (and
thank God there are many) thinks God's thoughts after
him.

A PREPARATORY ACTION.

God's act of creation was not an end in itself, but the first
step in space and time in the fulfilment of the covenant of
redemption, the Triune God's eternal plan of salvation.
Scripture clearly shows that this plan was included in the

[14] A. A. Hodge, *Evangelical Theology* (Edinburgh: Banner of Truth,
1976), pp. 22–3.

eternal counsel of God. Paul speaks of 'the eternal purpose that he [the Father] has realized in Christ Jesus our
Lord, in whom we have boldness and access with confidence through our faith in him' (*Eph*.3:11; cf. 2 *Tim*.1:9;
James 2:5). The covenant of redemption and the covenant
of grace are two phases of the same eternal covenant of
mercy, the covenant of grace being the outworking in time
of God's eternal plan of salvation. In the Old Testament
the teaching of the prophets concerning creation centres
on the hope of new heavens and a new earth. The same is
true of the New Testament.

Unlike the current suggestions of so many unbelieving
scientists, Scripture never sees the end of this earth in
terms of catastrophe and extinction. On the contrary, a
glorious future is predicted for a purged and renewed
earth (2 *Pet*. 3:11–13). From the beginning creation
looked forward to this grand climax.

Embraced in God's cosmic plan is the comprehensive
salvation of the Lord's elect: they await that glorious day
and are careful to order their lives accordingly (2 *Pet*.
3:14). Consequently, they will see and enjoy that 'new
earth'. Creation, then, set the stage for the fulfilment of
the 'mother-promise' of Genesis 3:15. Christ would crush
the serpent's head, signalling the utter defeat of Satan, the
enemy of God and his creation.

Too often Christians fail to see creation in this redemptive context. But, as Robert L. Reymond points out:

> In his eternal purpose God intentionally integrated both
> the purpose of creation as well as the ordinance of
> creation into the primary redemptive plan which he

accomplished in Christ . . . Creation's *raison d'être* then is to serve the redemptive ends of God.[15]

The first creation and the 'new creation that Christ will establish, are linked in the mind and purpose of God. The salvation of God's chosen ones is to be seen in that context. 'For God who said, "Let light shine out of darkness", has shone in our hearts the light of the knowledge of the glory of God in the face of Jesus Christ' (2 *Cor.* 4:6).

Even though little separate attention is paid to the creation of man in Paul's epistles . . . this fact for Paul is so fundamental and self-evident that any doubting of it would make his whole gospel unintelligible (cf. *1 Cor.* 8:6; *Rom.* 11:36). It is also in harmony with this that Paul speaks of the man in Christ as 'a new creation' . . . which in the nature of the case presupposes his original creation by God.[16]

With the entrance of sin, the harmony of creation was shattered and a discordant note prevailed. Tranquillity and peace were replaced by antagonism and conflict. All nature shared in the curse entailed by man's fall (*Gen.* 3:17-18).

The animals no longer enjoyed, under a mild rule, such happiness as they were capable of, but were transformed into ravenous beasts of prey, to be destroyed lest they

[15] Robert L. Reymond, *A New Systematic Theology of the Christian Faith* (Nashville: Thomas Nelson Publishers, 1998), p. 396-7.
[16] Herman Ridderbos, *Paul: An Outline of his Theology* (Grand Rapids: Wm. B. Eerdmans, 1975), p. 105.

should overrun the earth, or into slaves of a tyrannical master . . . Now, if the earth is to be the scene of paradise regained, it is necessary that a reversal of the curse take place. New heavens and a new earth must supersede the old, otherwise there would be a discrepancy between the glorified Church and its local environment. Such is the strain of ancient prophecy . . . [17]

This final day of redemption was in Christ's mind when he spoke of 'the new world' ('the renewal' or 'regeneration', *palingenesis, Matt.*19:28). Clearly we are to look beyond the present fallen world-order to the coming state of bliss and perfection in a renewed earth. '"What no eye has seen, nor ear heard, nor the heart of man imagined, what God has prepared for those who love him" – these things God has revealed to us through the Spirit' (*1 Cor.* 2:9–10).

This prophetic expectation was buoyant. 'For behold, I create new heavens and a new earth, and the former things shall not be remembered or come into mind. But be glad and rejoice for ever in that which I create; for behold, I create Jerusalem to be a joy, and her people to be a gladness' (*Isa.* 65:17–18). The reversal of the curse (*Rev.* 22:3) and the cosmic renewal are the results of Christ's cross, his redemptive suffering, by which Satan and his legions were routed, and their efforts to annihilate God's creation defeated. Sentence may be suspended, but Satan and his forces know the doom that awaits them.

[17] E. A. Litton, *Introduction to Dogmatic Theology* (London, James Clarke, 1960), p. 600.

The demons said to Christ, 'Have you come here to torment us before the time?' (*Matt.* 8:29), and in Revelation 12:12 we read that 'the devil . . . knows that his time is short.'

The cross of Christ is central in the mind and heart of the eternal God (*Rev.*13:8); the cross is central in the outworking of redemption in history (*Col.* 2:14–15); the cross is central in the experience of salvation (*Gal.* 6:14) and the cross is central in the worship of the redeemed in glory (*Rev.* 5:11–14).

In the coming day when creation is restored and enhanced, God will be glorified; even now his glory surrounds us, whether we contemplate the incomprehensible vastness of the universe or the microscopic wonders of the most minute organism. In Hebrews 11:3 we read, 'By faith we understand that the universe was created by the word of God.' This *we understand*. This is not the product of speculation or guess-work or credulity. It is by faith – a faith enlightened by the Word of God, which in itself is a lamp to our feet and a light to our path (*Psa.* 119:105). We either exercise this light-induced faith in God and his Word or a blind faith in a man-made theory. In the latter case there is no certainty, no comfort, and no hope.[18]

[18] See Appendix B.

2

THE HAND THAT GOVERNS

The Asian Tsunami of December 2004 shook the world. Hundreds of thousands drowned. The devastation on land and sea in several countries was staggering. History records equally horrendous disasters: the Black Death (1347–9), which ravaged Europe killing some 25 million people; the Holocaust, in which some 6 million people, mostly Jews, were brutally exterminated by Hitler's henchmen.

When considering these and similar disasters, we need to remember our Lord's words about 'the Galileans whose blood Pilate had mingled with their sacrifices . . . [and] those eighteen on whom the tower in Siloam fell and killed them': 'Do you think', asked Christ, 'that they were worse offenders than all the others who lived in Jerusalem? No, I tell you, but unless you repent, you will all likewise perish' (*Luke* 13:1–5). All are guilty, and those who do not repent will face a far greater 'disaster'.

At the time of the Tsunami, questions were asked about God. Was this an 'act of God' or a divine judgment? More than once a church leader was heard to say on news bulletins and broadcast discussions that 'God had nothing to do with it.' The implications of such a statement are profound. It is tantamount to saying that God is not in full control of creation. It is more in keeping with the Deistic idea of an aloof God, the 'absentee landlord' who, having made the universe, left it to function on its own, taking no active part in its movements.

All such events and questions lead to a consideration of the sovereignty of God, a truth that the Bible proclaims in the most emphatic terms: an all-knowing, all-powerful God has absolute dominion over his creation. 'The earth is the LORD's and the fullness thereof, the world and those who dwell therein' (*Psa.* 24:1). For God is the King of all the earth' (*Psa.*47:7). The sovereignty of God is a pervasive theme in Scripture, and in the sacred narrative we see frequent examples of God's rule: the deliverance of the Israelites from Egypt; the supplying of food and water for his people in the wilderness, the collapsing of the walls of Jericho, Christ's feeding of four and five thousand with a few small loaves and fish.

When the Christian speaks of the sovereignty of God, the atheist shakes his head and smiles: 'Do you live in the real world?' he asks. 'Do you ever read a newspaper or watch the news?' 'Either this God of yours is a cruel, heartless tyrant, or so feeble that he is not able to govern.' The atheist's words reveal a profound ignorance of the facts: the fact that the earth is under a curse because of man's sin (*Gen.*3:17); the fact of Satan, the enemy of God and man, who is likened to 'a roaring lion' (*1 Pet.* 5:8), the fact of man's sinful behaviour to his fellow-man, the fact that by the cross of Christ Satan's time is limited and that in due course (God's time, not ours) evil will be banished from the universe. The atheist denies these facts, although most of them are staring him in the face, and so he walks in the darkness of his unbelief.

It cannot be stressed too strongly that the sovereignty of God is all-embracing. John Murray writes:

> It is possible for us to profess the sovereignty of God and deny it in the particulars in which this sovereignty is expressed, to assert a universal but evade the particularities.[1]

The statement of the *Westminster Confession* that 'God from all eternity, did, by the most wise and holy counsel of His own will, freely and unchangeably ordain whatsoever comes to pass' (III:1) is unacceptable to the modern mind, and many Christians also find it hard to accept. The *Confession* makes it clear that God is not the author of evil and that 'no violence is offered to the will of the creatures'. Much of the evil in this world is Satanic in origin, and for the present, God in his longsuffering patience permits such a world to exist. What God allows, he wills.

God affirms his sovereignty unequivocally:

> I am God, and there is no other; I am God, and there is none like me, declaring the end from the beginning and from ancient times things not yet done, saying, 'My counsel shall stand, and I will accomplish all my purpose . . . I have spoken, and I will do it' (*Isa.* 46:9–11).

Here speaks the One whose ways are higher than our ways 'as the heavens are higher than the earth', and

[1] *Collected Writings*, vol. 4, p. 191.

whose thoughts are higher than our thoughts (*Isa.* 55:8–9). Before such an affirmation of absolute, unshakeable sovereignty the Christian should exclaim with the apostle Paul, 'Oh, the depth of the riches and wisdom and knowledge of God! How unsearchable are his judgements and how inscrutable his ways!' (*Rom.* 11:33). Oh, the depth! Calvin's comment on that verse is as superb as it is salutary:

> This expression of wonder ought greatly to avail to the beating down of the presumption of our flesh, for after having spoken from the word and by the Spirit of the Lord, being at length overcome by the sublimity of so great a mystery, he could not do otherwise than wonder and exclaim, that the riches of God's wisdom are deeper than our reason can penetrate to. Whenever, then, we enter on a discourse respecting the eternal counsels of God, let a bridle be always set on our thoughts and tongue, so that after having spoken soberly and within the limits of God's word, our reasoning may at last end in admiration.[2]

In recent decades, an aberration of the doctrine of God's sovereignty, a dangerous hybrid known as 'the open view of God', has attracted a number of professedly evangelical theologians. It represented God as sharing power with man, becoming 'vulnerable' and taking 'risks'. It is blatantly contrary to the plain teaching of Scripture.[3]

---

[2] John Calvin, *Commentary on the Epistle of Paul to the Romans* (Grand Rapids: Wm. B. Eerdmans, 1955), p. 444.

[3] See Appendix C.

GOD'S CONTROL OF NATURE

In our everyday speech we tend to say 'It is raining' or 'It is snowing': the ancient Hebrews, however, said that God sent rain and snow and lightning. 'Rain in abundance, O God, you shed abroad' (*Psa.* 68:9). God said to Israel, 'If you walk in my statutes and observe my commandments and do them, then I will give you your rains in their season' (*Lev.* 26:3–4). There was a day when the prophet Samuel said to the people, 'Is it not wheat harvest today? I will call upon the LORD, that he may send thunder and rain. And you shall know and see that your wickedness is great.' And 'Samuel called on the LORD, and the LORD sent thunder and rain that day' (*1 Sam.* 12:17–18).

In the Old Testament, God speaks as the Lord of nature, and his people understood this from his Word. There are so many impressive examples of God's complete control of the forces of nature. We think of the Flood by which God judged a violent and corrupt earth (*Gen.* 6:12); of God driving back the Red Sea 'by a strong east wind all night', so that Israel could cross over on dry land (*Exod.* 14:21); of the time when God caused a wind to bring quail from the sea to the camp of Israel (*Num.* 11:31); of God sending a drought by the word of Elijah in the days of Ahab and later, by the word of this same prophet, sending rain (*1 Kings* 17:1; 18:1). So many similar examples can be given.

Then, in the New Testament, we see Jesus, the God-man, 'rebuking' the wind and saying to the sea 'Peace! be still!' In the ensuing calm, the disciples exclaimed, 'Who then is this, that even wind and sea obey him?' (*Mark*

4:39–41). William Lane comments that 'The cosmic over-
tones in the Gospel account must not be missed', and
adds, 'The force of the sea was muzzled as Jesus subdued
it with his sovereign word of authority.'[4]

God is no absentee sovereign and nature is not a closed,
self-sufficient system. God is present and active in nature:
he constantly preserves and governs his creation. He declares, 'I am the LORD, and there is no other. I form light
and create darkness' (*Isa.* 45:7). Clearly he is above and
distinct from creation while meaningfully engaged with it.
In a world where it was and still is common for pagans to
worship nature-gods or heavenly bodies, the ancient Jews
were preserved by God's self-revelation from Pantheism,
which failed to distinguish between the Creator and
creation. The worship of sun, moon and stars was expressly forbidden (*Deut.* 4:19).

A secular society that in thought has removed the
Creator from his creation, has suffered the loss of both a
coherent and orderly concept of nature, and a sense of
purpose in history. When nature is considered in isolation
from God, the end result is meaninglessness, if not chaos.
That is the bleak inheritance this generation has received
from its unbelieving forebears who refused to acknowledge the 'hand of God' in nature. The truth stated in
Nehemiah 9:6 must ever be confessed: 'You are the LORD,
you alone. You have made heaven, the heaven of heavens,
with all their host, the earth and all that is in it, the seas
and all that is in them; and you preserve all of them' (cf.

---

[4] William Lane, *The Gospel according to Mark* (London: Marshall
Morgan & Scott, 1974), p. 177.

Job 5:10; *Psa.* 104:3, 19). The *Belgic Confession* affirms that

> God after He had created all things, did not forsake them, nor give them to fortune or chance, but that He rules and governs them according to His holy will, so that nothing happens in this world without His appointment (Article XIII).

Nowhere does God declare his sovereignty over his creation more strongly or sublimely than in his address to Job (38–41). Though he speaks in awesome majesty in these chapters, Job was not confronted by an impersonal, irresistible force, but by the hand of a loving heavenly Father (cf. *James* 5:11).

Nothing in nature is static. There is constant change, and yet there is underlying regularity and stability as promised and guaranteed by the covenant God confirmed to Noah after the Flood (*Gen.* 9). Where does this uniformity in nature come from, if not from God who, through his Son, 'upholds the universe by the word of his power' (*Heb.* 1:3).

What a comfort to know that this universe, including man, is not a meaningless, purposeless, mindless mass, but the creation of the Triune God, reflecting his wisdom and glory and whose every movement is controlled by him.

As his Word joyfully declares:

> He sends out his command to the earth; his word runs swiftly. He gives snow like wool; he scatters hoarfrost like ashes. He hurls down his crystals of ice like crumbs;

who can stand before his cold? He sends out his word
and melts them; he makes his wind blow and the waters
flow (*Psa.* 147:15–18).

No wonder the Psalm closes with a 'Hallelujah', which
we should all repeat.

GOD'S CONTROL OF HISTORY

G. M. Trevelyan concludes his masterly *History of England* thus: 'Of the future the historian can see no more
than others. He can only point like a showman to the
things of the past, with their manifold and mysterious
message.'[5] The Bible, on the other hand, tells us why and
how history began and where it is going. History is not a
haphazard series of events: it is divinely ordained and
controlled with a definite purpose in view. Old Testament
history is prophetic. By types and symbols it points to
Christ and his kingdom. The cross of Christ is central in
all of history, and therefore it is true to say that Christianity is embedded in history.

To surrender God's redemptive activity in history would
be to forfeit the Christian faith. We cannot lift Christianity out of history as liberal theologians tend to do. As J.
Gresham Machen wrote, 'Christianity depends, not upon
a complex of ideas, but upon the narrative of an event.' In
another place he argues that 'a gospel independent of history is a contradiction in terms.'[6] The gospel is 'good

---

[5] G. M. Trevelyan, *History of England* (London: Longman, Green &
Co., 1962 edition), p. 734.
[6] *Christianity and Liberalism* (New York: Macmillan, 1924), pp. 70,
121.

news' and Machen ably demonstrated how this good news is 'an account of something that happened'. When 'the meaning of the happening was set forth, then there was Christian doctrine . . . "Christ died" – that is history; "Christ died for our sins" – that is doctrine.'[7]

Since the cross is pivotal in all of history, it follows that God is in control of history. The polytheistic religions pit one deity against another. The Bible relates all history to the one and only God. As Carl Henry remarked: 'Elijah knew that the issue at Carmel was God *or* Baal, not God *and* Baal.'[8]

The Old Testament teems with examples of God's control of history. The opening words of the book of Daniel are striking: 'In the third year of the reign of Jehoiakim king of Judah, Nebuchadnezzar king of Babylon came to Jerusalem and besieged it. And the Lord gave Jehoiakim king of Judah into his hand' (*Dan.* 1:1–2). If the political analysts of today had been on earth then, we can imagine how they would have considered preceding events and policies and prognosticated about the future; all on the horizontal. The vertical, 'the hand of God', would never have entered their minds. At the time of the Babylonian exile believing Jews, conscious of God's hand in history, might well have been tempted to think that God had been tragically defeated by a pagan power. In fact, to resist the Babylonian armies would have been to resist the will of God. By his prophet Jeremiah, who foretold this event, God had described Nebuchadnezzar as his 'servant'. God's warning had been clear:

---

[7] Ibid. p. 27.   [8] Op. cit., vol. 2, p. 9.

Because you have not obeyed my words, behold, I will send for all the tribes of the north, declares the Lord, and for Nebuchadnezzar the king of Babylon, my servant, and I will bring them against all these surrounding nations . . . This whole land shall become a ruin and a waste, and these nations shall serve the king of Babylon seventy years. Then after seventy years are completed, I will punish the king of Babylon and that nation . . . for their iniquity, declares the Lord' (*Jer.* 25:8–14).

God's word through Jeremiah was fulfilled to the letter. Calvin comments:

Nebuchadnezzar thought that he was making war with the God of Israel when he invaded Judea; and only ambition, and avarice, and cruelty impelled him to undertake so many wars. When, therefore, we think of him, of his designs and projects, we cannot say that he was God's servant; but this is to be referred to God only, who governs by his hidden and incomprehensible power both the devil and the ungodly, so that they execute, though unwittingly, whatever he determines.[9]

In all of this, there was no fortuitous turn of events. Cyrus, king of Persia, who conquered Babylon and issued a decree permitting the Jews to return to their own land (*Ezra* 1:1–11), is described as God's 'anointed', 'whose right hand I have grasped to subdue nations before him (*Isa.* 45:1). And Ezra states that 'the Lord stirred up the spirit of Cyrus . . . so that he made a

[9] John Calvin, *Commentary on Jeremiah* (Edinburgh: Banner of Truth, 1989), vol. 3, p. 252.

proclamation throughout all his kingdom and also put it in writing' (*Ezra* 1:1).

We can also think of Joseph, so callously treated by his brethren, saying to them years later, 'You meant evil against me, but God meant it for good (*Gen.* 50:20; cf. 2 *Sam.* 17:14). God makes the wrath of man to praise him (*Psa.* 76:10). In more recent times American scientists, engaged in the making of the first atomic bomb, were concerned that Germany might develop this awful weapon first, in which event Hitler would not have hesitated to use it. At the close of the War, however, it was discovered that Germany was well behind in the nuclear race, for Hitler did not deign to use Jewish scientists!

The outstanding and unique example of God's sovereign control of history is the crucifixion of Christ, in itself a wicked deed. Yet Peter, in Acts 2:23, declared to the people of Jerusalem, 'This Jesus, delivered up according to the definite plan and foreknowledge of God, you crucified and killed by the hands of lawless men.' God had directed all history to that hour when 'the mother-promise' of Genesis 3:15 would be fulfilled. Klaas Schilder puts it so well:

> God has arranged all of the preceding centuries, all of the intervolutions of time, all of the events from Genesis 1:1 up to this moment – has arranged, has moulded them, has had them converge in such a way that there would be a place for this hour, the hour in which His Son will be bound. . . . He allowed neither the forces above nor the forces below to tamper with the clock of

history. He directed the battles of Caesars, the conflicts of kings, the migration of peoples, the world wars, the courses of stars and sun and moon, the change of epochs, and the complex movements of all things in the world in such a way that this hour had to come.[10]

GOD'S CONTROL OF EVIL

Sin is not a popular word: psychologists and sociologists, on the whole, do not like it; liberal preachers never mention it. Yet it is still common to speak of wickedness and cruelty and corruption, all of which are in breach of God's law, and therefore covered by the word sin: 'Sin is the transgression of the law' (*1 John* 3:4, KJV). Liberals speak of the inherent goodness of man and express a confidence in human nature. Yet the Bible teaches that human nature is inherently corrupt and that the totality of man's being is depraved: every faculty, such as reason, will, emotions and imagination, are contaminated by sin. 'The heart is deceitful above all things, and desperately sick; who can understand it? I the LORD search the heart and test the mind' (*Jer.*17:9).

The Lutheran Hebrew scholar, Theodore Laetsch, translates Jeremiah 17:9 as follows: 'The heart is treacherous above all things, and incurable.' He further comments: 'In point of deceitfulness, treachery, the human heart exceeds all things. And the greatest deception it has conceived is the lie of the natural goodness of man's heart . . . This

[10] Klaus Schilder, *Christ in His Suffering* (Grand Rapids: Wm. B. Eerdmans, 1945), p. 437.

treacherous lie is the greatest obstacle to a humble return to God.'[11]

The mind of sinful man is enmity against God, 'for it is not subject to the law of God, neither indeed can be' (*Rom.* 8:7, KJV). Man's fallen nature is governed by enmity towards God. Therefore the apostle concludes that 'they that are in the flesh cannot please God' (*Rom.* 8:8). Satan reigns in the heart of man who has followed the devil's way. This world has made Satan its god (2 *Cor.* 4:4), and, as W. G. T. Shedd says, 'Satan cannot cast out Satan.'[12] We see, then, that man's sinful nature is inherently opposed to God, and self-recovery is impossible.

Evolutionists prefer to see evil as a remnant of the brute instinct, something to be gradually eradicated by education, social reforms, and such like. Such a view of evil is another of Satan's lies and is contrary both to Scripture and human experience.

A frequently overlooked aspect of the work of the Holy Spirit is his restraint of evil in this world. Unrestrained, sin intensifies and its horrifying consequences know no bounds. 'Evil people and impostors will go on from bad to worse, deceiving and being deceived' (2 *Tim.* 3:13), which suggests a steady progression in evil: the law of increase by exercise applies to evil as well as to good.

A sovereign God, with a people to save throughout many centuries, does not allow this world to sink so low

[11] Theodore Laetsch, *Jeremiah* (Saint Louis: Concordia Publishing House, 1952), p. 163.

[12] W. G. T. Shedd *Commentary on Romans* (Grand Rapids: Baker Book House, 1980), p. 235.

that his purpose cannot be realized. Were it not for the restraining power of his Spirit, society would disintegrate in a matter of hours. That restraint of the Spirit makes it possible for home, society, and civilization to exist. When, in a measure, that influence was withdrawn from Pharaoh, God 'hardened' his heart. Often the dangerous passions of men are curbed, as when God averted the rage of Esau against Jacob. All earthly good rests upon the Holy Spirit's grand and gracious restraint of sin. One of the chief horrors of hell will be the absence of that restraint: such endless deterioration is dreadful to contemplate.[13]

GOD'S CONTROL OF HIS KINGDOM

God revealed himself to ancient Israel as King. After their deliverance at the Red Sea, the Hebrews sang, 'The LORD will reign for ever and ever' (*Exod.*15:18). When, in the course of time, they asked to have a king like the other nations, their request was seen as an offence to Jehovah. To Samuel God said, 'They have not rejected you, but they have rejected me from being king over them' (*1 Sam.* 8:7). At best, a human king was merely representative. Nevertheless, the thought of God's kingship dominates the Old Testament Scriptures. It is a recurring theme in the Psalms.

This rule of heaven and kingship of Jehovah was the

---

[13] There is an excellent discussion of this aspect of the Holy Spirit's work in C. R. Vaughan's *The Gifts of the Holy Spirit* (Edinburgh: Banner of Truth, 1975), chapter 1.

very substance of the Old Testament; the object of the calling and mission of Israel; the meaning of all its ordinances, whether civil or religious; the underlying idea of all its institutions. It explained alike the history of the people, the dealings of God with them, and the prospects opened up by the prophets. Without it the Old Testament could not be understood; it gave perpetuity to its teaching, and dignity to its representations. . . Thus the whole Old Testament was the preparatory presentation of the rule of heaven and of the Kingship of its Lord.[14]

The coming Messiah was seen as King and the glory of his reign was uppermost in the minds and hearts of prophets and poets. They saw the Messiah's coming as the dawn of the age of fulfilment. Isaiah spoke of the coming Messiah as sitting on 'the throne of David and over his kingdom to establish it and to uphold it with justice and with righteousness from this time forth and for evermore' (*Isa.* 9:7). The angel Gabriel, announcing the Saviour's birth to Mary, said, 'And the Lord God will give to him the throne of his father David, and he will reign over the house of Jacob for ever, and of his kingdom there will be no end' (*Luke* 1:32–33). It is important to remember that in the Old Testament God's reign was depicted as a kingdom of grace as well as of law, a balance preserved in Christ's teaching (cf. *Exod.* 34:6–8 and *Luke* 1:78–79). Sadly, at the time of the Saviour's birth, the Jews had lost the spiritual vision of the prophets, and had come to think

---

[14] Alfred Edersheim, *The Life and Times of Jesus the Messiah* (Peabody: Hendrickson Publishers, 1997), p. 183 f.

of the Messiah's reign in earthly and political terms. There was indeed a believing remnant like Simeon who was 'waiting for the consolation of Israel' – that is, the salvation to come through the Messiah (*Luke* 2:25). Then there was Joseph of Arimathea who was 'looking for the kingdom of God' (*Mark* 15:43). But the attitude of the Jewish leaders was one of rejection. They would neither enter the kingdom themselves 'nor allow those who would enter to go in' (*Matt.* 23:14).

Our Lord saw the kingdom as a present reality: 'If it is by the Spirit of God that I cast out demons, then the kingdom of God has come upon you' (*Matt.* 12:28). Yet he also saw the full realization of the kingdom as a future event; and so he taught us to pray, 'Your kingdom come, your will be done on earth as it is in heaven' (*Matt.* 6:10). This is why Christian theologians make a distinction between the 'already' and the 'not yet'. In this life we are concerned with the present reality of the kingdom and what that entails, while anticipating the glorious consummation of the kingdom, which will only take place at Christ's return. 'At present, we do not yet see everything in subjection to him. But we see Jesus . . . crowned with glory and honour' (*Heb.* 2:9).

The church is central in the outworking of the kingdom. Christ said to Nicodemus, 'Truly, truly, I say to you, unless one is born again he cannot see the kingdom of God (*John* 3:3). The kingdom, then, is constituted by the regenerate, and so in the church we see the true nature and inner essence of the kingdom. The Lord Jesus Christ rules in the hearts and lives of believers.

In fact, an analysis of 119 passages in the New Testament where the expression 'kingdom' occurs shows that it means *the rule of God*, which was *manifested in and through Christ; is apparent in the church; gradually develops amidst hindrances; is triumphant at the second coming of Christ* ('the end'); and, finally, *is perfected in the world to come.*[15]

That kingdom of grace is our portion now. Already it is present: 'The kingdom of God is in the midst of you.' So said the Saviour to unbelieving Pharisees. He went through 'all the cities and villages . . . proclaiming the gospel of the kingdom' (*Matt.* 9:35), and in Ephesus, the apostle Paul 'entered the synagogue and for three months spoke boldly, reasoning and persuading them about the kingdom of God' (*Acts* 19:8, cf. *Acts* 8:12). What place, we may ask, does the kingdom – the reign of Christ – God's anointed King, have in today's preaching of the gospel? In our Lord's preaching and in that of the apostolic church it was central.

The Bible speaks of two kingdoms in opposition to one another, that of God and that of the usurper Satan, whom the world has made its 'prince' (*John* 12:31, KJV). God 'has delivered us from the domain of darkness and transferred us to the kingdom of his beloved Son, in whom we have redemption, the forgiveness of sins' (*Col.* 1:13–14). This 'jurisdiction of darkness' is Satan's realm.[16] Christ,

---

[15] Alfred Edersheim, *Life and Times*, p. 187.

[16] It is noteworthy that this expression occurs in Luke's account of our Lord's arrest in Gethsemane, where he said to his captors, 'This is your hour and the jurisdiction of darkness.' (*Luke* 22:52f.).

by his victory on the cross, raids this evil domain and rescues those imprisoned in it, transferring them to his own kingdom. Everyone, without exception, belongs either to one or other of these two kingdoms. This fact is supremely relevant to the preaching of the gospel, but, again we ask, what place does it have in today's evangelical preaching? Too much contemporary preaching seldom rises above 'See what Jesus can do for you', as if God existed for the sake of man!

The Second Psalm graphically depicts the hostility of a fallen world to the LORD's anointed King. But it also shows the world's impotence in its efforts to unseat him and prophesies the rebellious world's ultimate and crushing defeat. Yet even as this judgment is being foretold, the call to repentance is sounded forth.

While in the church we see the essence or the essential nature of the kingdom (and we cannot be in the kingdom if we are not members of the church that Christ 'obtained with his own blood', *Acts* 20:28), nevertheless God's kingdom, in the broadest sense of the term, extends beyond the jurisdiction of the church, although not beyond its witness. God's reign pervades every aspect of human life. There are distinct spheres of human activity, such as the home, the school, the state, science, art, commerce, and politics (see following chart). However, there ought to be no sphere upon whose door the notice is hung, 'No Admittance' to God. Yes, it is true that the world often displays that sign, but that is its sin, its shame, and its condemnation. In everything Christ should have the pre-eminence (*Col.* 1:18). It is not the function of the church to meddle in other spheres of human activity, but it is duty bound to be a witness and to proclaim the 'Crown Rights of King Jesus'. Individual members of the church should exert a God-glorifying influence in their various spheres of work and so 'shine as lights in the world' (*Phil.* 2:15). God's cause cannot fail. Our divine Saviour has 'all authority in heaven and on earth' (*Matt.* 28:18), and one glorious day loud voices will declare, 'The kingdom of the world has become the kingdom of our Lord and of his Christ, and he shall reign for ever and ever' (*Rev.*11:15). God is one: '*He* shall reign for ever and ever.' In a troubled and dangerous world, God's people can live in peace knowing that their Redeemer reigns. There can be no greater privilege or honour for a man or a woman than to be a citizen of the kingdom of God.

> When God says to me 'obey', then I humbly bow my head, without compromising in the least my personal dignity, as a man. For, in like proportion as you degrade yourself, by bowing low to a child of man, whose breath is in his nostrils; so, on the other hand do you raise yourself, if you submit to the authority of the Lord of heaven and earth
>
> *Abraham Kuyper*[17]

[17] Abraham Kuyper, *Calvinism* (London: Sovereign Grace Union, 1932), p. 131.

CHURCH AND KINGDOM

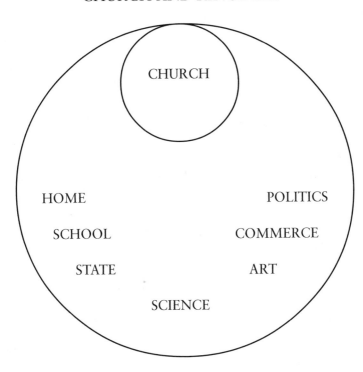

We become members of the kingdom by the 'new birth' (*John* 3:3); and so in the church we see the essential nature of the kingdom. Nevertheless, this kingdom, in the broadest sense of the term, extends to include every sphere of human activity (*Col* 1:18).

3

THE HAND THAT PROVIDES

G od's provision for his people's needs comes, at times, from the most unexpected quarters. The Bible affords some graphic examples of this. When, in time of famine, Jacob heard that there was 'grain for sale in Egypt' (the KJV has 'corn in Egypt'), he said to his sons, 'Go down and buy grain for us there, that we may live and not die' (*Gen.* 42:1–2). Egypt was the last place where Jacob would have expected to find grain, for it was also struck by the drought; but Egypt's corn had been safely stockpiled by order of that nation's 'prime minister', Joseph! Commenting upon this story, Spurgeon says, 'Believer, though all things are apparently against thee, rest assured that God has made a reservation on thy behalf.'[1]

When at another time famine was widespread, God sent Elijah to Cherith, east of the Jordan. Elijah heard God say, 'You shall drink from the brook, and I have commanded the ravens to feed you there' (*1 Kings* 17:4). Ravens! The raven was an unclean bird according to God's law and was described as 'detestable' (*Lev.* 11:13–

[1] C. H. Spurgeon, *Morning and Evening* (London: Marshall, Morgan & Scott, 1966), p. 285.

15). Ravens are ravenous birds of prey, more likely to snatch food *from* Elijah than to bring it *to* the hungry prophet. God could have sent angels to minister to his servant, as he did later (*1 Kings* 19:5), but he chose to send the 'detested' raven, and Elijah had no qualms about enjoying the constant supply of food, each morning and evening. God 'commanded the ravens'; they were sovereignly appointed and directed by the 'hand of God'.

Then when the brook dried up, God told Elijah to go to Zarephath in Sidon, adding, 'Behold, I have commanded a widow there to feed you' (*1 Kings* 17:8). In that town Elijah found a widow gathering sticks so that she could prepare a last meal for herself and her son. All she had was 'a handful of flour in a jar and a little oil in a jug' (*1 Kings* 17:12). But Elijah asked for food, saying, 'The jar of food shall not be spent, and the jug of oil shall not be empty, until the LORD sends rain upon the earth' (*1 Kings* 17:14). And so it proved. So God sent his servant to a Gentile city and to a poor widow facing death along with her son.

This whole event was a foreshadowing of the blessing that God would yet bestow on the Gentiles. As our Lord said when on earth, 'I tell you, there were many widows in Israel in the days of Elijah . . . and a great famine came over the land, and Elijah was sent to none of them but only to Zarephath in the land of Sidon, to a woman who was a widow' (*Luke* 4:25–27). It is significant that Sidon was associated with the worship of Baal and was also the home town of wicked Queen Jezebel (*1 Kings* 16:31). Jezebel was Elijah's bitter enemy, yet the sovereign God found a place of refuge for him in her own back yard! We also note that in our Saviour's earthly ministry, he did not go to Gentile territory, except 'to the district of Tyre and Sidon' (*Matt.*15:21). Our Sovereign God can provide for his own in various and sometimes unexpected ways. This was something Elijah was to learn, and something we all must learn. 'Behold, the LORD's hand is not shortened that it cannot save, or his ear dull that it cannot hear' (*Isa.* 59:1).

PROVISION AND NEED

Scripture bears consistent witness to God's provision for the needs of all his creatures. Psalm 104 is an outstanding example of this testimony.

With reference to living creatures the Psalmist writes, 'These all look to you, to give them their food in due season. When you give it to them, they gather it up; when you open your hand, they are filled with good things' (*Psa.* 104:27–28). Apart from God's bountiful provision, no creature could exist.

His relationship to his creation is fatherly. He knows that we have many physical needs and he supplies them. He knows what we need before we ask him (*Matt.* 6:8).

We are not to be obsessed with thoughts about daily needs like food and clothing. Christ said, 'Your heavenly Father knows that you need them all.' As believers 'seek first the kingdom of God and his righteousness', he faithfully supplies their needs (*Matt.* 6:32). Leon Morris observes 'that it is need of which Jesus speaks. His followers may expect their needs to be met, but not necessarily their desires.'[2]

God is equally bountiful in supplying our spiritual needs: body and soul matter to him. In the light of this truth, Paul could write to the Philippian Christians, 'And my God will supply every need of yours according to his riches in glory in Christ Jesus' (*Phil.* 4:19). God supplies our *every need*, material and spiritual. He does so 'in Christ Jesus'. In the Saviour there is full provision for all the needs of his people. At times Christians have hard struggles, but that should be an inducement to draw near to God's throne of grace. There they 'receive mercy and find grace to help in time of need' (*Heb.* 4:16).

Prayer has a crucial role in the believer's experiencing all of God's provision. The Lord Jesus taught us to pray, 'Give us this day our daily bread' (*Matt.* 6:11). This, like the rest of 'the Lord's Prayer', is corporate: 'give *us*'. It is not a 'me and mine' prayer. As members of the body of Christ we should pray accordingly. So also in spiritual matters, we 'draw near' to the throne of grace in prayer. The promise is clear: 'Ask, and it will be given to you; seek, and you will find; knock, and it will be opened to you.' A kind earthly father, even though a sinner, will endeavour to give the best to his children who come to him with their requests; and Christ comments, 'how much more will your Father who is in heaven give good things to those who ask him!' (*Matt.* 7:7–11). Ask! Seek! Knock! In other words, Pray! Keep on praying! And don't give

[2] Leon Morris, *The Gospel according to Matthew* (Grand Rapids: Wm. B. Eerdmans, 1992), p. 161.

up! Matthew Henry says, 'You may as soon find a living man without breath as a living saint without prayer.'[3]

> Lord, what a change within us one short hour
> Spent in Thy presence will avail to make!
> What heavy burdens from our bosoms take;
> What parched grounds refresh as with a shower!
> We kneel, and all around us seems to lower;
> We rise, and all the distant and the near
> Stands forth in sunny outline, brave and clear.
> We kneel, how weak! We rise, how full of power!
> Why, therefore, should we do ourselves this wrong
> Or others, that, we are not always strong,
> That we are ever overborne with care,
> That we should ever weak or heartless be
> Anxious or troubled, when with us is prayer,
> And joy and strength and courage are with Thee?
> *Richard Chenevix Trench*

It has been well said that prayer is not the means by which we get from God what we want; rather it is a means God uses to give us what he wants. In Ezekiel 36:24–36 we have a series of glorious promises, spiritual and material, that God made to Israel. Then in verse 37 we hear God say, 'This also I will let the house of Israel ask me to do for them.' God uses the prayers that the Holy Spirit prompts to fulfil his purposes.

It is easy for Christians in the West to meet in their comfortable church buildings, praise God for his bountiful

---

[3] On Zechariah 12:9–10, in Matthew Henry's *Commentary on the Whole Bible*.

provisions, and count their blessings. What about the 'church under the cross'? Through the centuries, God's people have often experienced prolonged persecution. We think of the massacre of the Huguenots on St Bartholomew's Day (24 August 1572), celebrated by Pope Gregory XIII who struck a medal with the inscription, *Ugonottorum strages* (slaughter of the Huguenots). One of the most cruel of many persecutions was the murderous campaign against the Waldenses of the Piedmont valleys (1655), which called forth a strong protest from Oliver Cromwell. His Foreign Secretary, the Puritan John Milton, was moved to write:

> Avenge, O Lord, thy slaughtered saints, whose bones
> Lie scattered on the Alpine mountains cold,
> Ev'n them who kept thy truth so pure of old,
> When all our fathers worshipped stocks and stones.

It was in such times that the church saw the courageous testimony of her noblest sons and daughters, men and women of unflinching loyalty to Christ. This was true of the Covenanters in Scotland, the Huguenots in France, and the Waldenses – 'the Israel of the Alps'. The English martyrs in the reign of Queen Mary (1553–8) were staunch, some even jubilant as they went to the stake. When Ridley and Latimer, Bishops of the Church of England, were chained back to back at the same stake, and the fire was lit at Ridley's feet, Latimer said to his fellow sufferer for Christ's gospel, 'Be of good cheer, Master Ridley, and play the man; we shall this day light such a candle, by God's grace, in England, as I trust shall never be put out.' That candle still burns, somewhat dimly today perhaps; but what God did in sixteenth-century England, he can do again. History shows that the church is at her brightest and best in times of persecution: the Lord walks in fellowship with his own amidst the flames.

In this twenty-first century, Christians in several lands continue to face persecution. They have been imprisoned, tortured, killed, and had their buildings burned to the ground. Yet they faithfully maintain their witness to the truth. Mere formal professions of faith would not endure such circumstances. May we stand with our persecuted brethren in prayer.

God's goodness and bounty extends far beyond the bounds of his church. 'The LORD is good to all, and his mercy is over all he has made' (*Psa.* 145:9). What, then do we say to the millions who are homeless, lacking food and water, medication and sanitation, the refugees of war-torn lands who have been raped, tortured, and plunged into heart-wrenching misery? Thousands more suffer as the result of flood, famine and storm. Millions are victims of AIDS, including infants born on the threshold of the grave.

We see a broken, suffering world. There is so much exploitation, injustice and barbarity. Strong men despair; broken-hearted women weep; traumatized young people cannot weep, and thousands of children die every day from starvation, malnutrition, and disease. In 2005 it was estimated that 13,700 children died from hunger related conditions every day, a rate of one child death every seven seconds! This is not empty rhetoric; it is cold fact. And all of this takes place in an age when man boasts of his scientific and technological achievements!

What does Christ's church say and do in such a fallen world? We do not have all the answers, but Scripture does offer us some. Much human suffering in this world is caused by man's ill-treatment of his fellow-man. Sin lies at the heart of the human problem. We know, too, that Satan and his legions are constantly active, bent on disorder and strife. Suffering humanity needs to hear the truth about this world, and to be told of the Christ in whom salvation is to be found, who has sealed Satan's doom, and who is coming to judge the world and to obliterate Satan's kingdom. Only in him can mankind find hope and comfort in a fallen world, bearing the curse entailed by sin and battered relentlessly by the forces of evil. The church must proclaim the gospel in all the world, and Christians must show the love of God by good works and the practical support of those in need. When the disciples suggested to Christ that he send the crowd he had been teaching to the villages so that they could 'buy themselves something to eat', he replied, 'You give them something to eat', and he miraculously enabled them to do so (*Matt.* 14:16). 'He simply turns their attention away from the hopelessness of the situation and their easy solution and invites them to think how they could help' (Leon Morris).[4]

PROVISION AND WORK

The quails and ravens God sent at different times to Israel and Elijah to supply them with food were unusual

[4] Leon Morris, *Matthew*, p. 378.

examples of God's provision. In the Bible such remarkable events were the exception and not the normal rule. When Adam was placed in Eden he was told to 'work it and keep it' (*Gen.* 2:15).

> The earth was given to man, with this condition, that he should occupy himself in its cultivation. Whence it follows, that men were created to employ themselves in some work, and not to lie down in inactivity and idleness. This labour, truly, was pleasant, and full of delight, entirely exempt from all trouble and weariness; since, however, God ordained that man should be exercised in the culture of the ground, he condemned in his person, all indolent repose
>
> John Calvin[5]

That is a recurring note throughout the Bible. We must work for physical and spiritual enrichment. It is not that God's gifts can be earned, but neither are they automatically provided. In this respect we also need to be aware of an unwarranted distinction between the 'spiritual' and the 'secular'. Alfred Edersheim puts it neatly when he says: 'To the spiritual man nothing is secular, and to the secular man nothing is spiritual.'[6] However, we may distinguish between the physical and the spiritual, provided that we do not press the distinction too far, because many forms of physical activity are evil.

[5] John Calvin, *Commentary on Genesis* (London: Banner of Truth, 1965), p. 125.

[6] Alfred Edersheim, *Sketches of Jewish Social Life* (Peabody: Hendrickson, 1994) p. 170.

It is truly impressive how the Bible stresses the need to work in order to have food and clothing and to sustain our earthly life. Laziness is condemned in the strongest possible terms, nowhere more frequently than in the book of Proverbs. 'Whoever works his land will have plenty of bread, but he who follows worthless pursuits will have plenty of poverty' (*Prov.* 28:19).

Go to the ant, O sluggard, consider her ways and be wise. Without having any chief officer, or ruler, she prepares her bread in summer and gathers her food in harvest. How long will you lie there, O sluggard? When will you arise from your sleep? A little sleep, a little slumber, a little folding of the hands to rest, and poverty will come upon you like a robber, and want like an armed man (*Prov.* 6:6–11).

There is a marked difference between sloth and anxiety about the future. Christ's word is salutary:

Therefore I tell you, do not be anxious about your life, what you will eat or what you will drink, nor about your body, what you will put on. Is not life more than food, and the body more than clothing? Look at the birds of the air: they neither sow nor reap nor gather into barns, and yet your heavenly Father feeds them. Are you not of more value than they? (*Matt.* 6:25–26)

This old fable in verse still carries a relevant message for us in this day of frantic getting.

Said the Sparrow to the Robin,
I should really like to know

> Why these anxious human beings
> Rush about and worry so.
>
> Said the Robin to the Sparrow,
> Friend, I think that it must be
> That they have no heavenly Father
> Such as cares for you and me.

Total dependence on God to supply our daily needs does not excuse idleness, which the New Testament condemns in even stronger terms than the Old. Paul wrote to Timothy, 'If anyone does not provide for his relatives, and especially for members of his household, he has denied the faith and is worse than an unbeliever' (*1 Tim.* 5:8). The converted thief must now resist the temptation to steal and instead must 'labour, doing honest work with his own hands, so that he may have something to share with anyone in need' (*Eph.* 4:28). E. K. Simpson terms this 'sterling honesty and wise generosity'.[7] To the Thessalonian Christians, Paul gave this stark rule: 'If anyone is not willing to work, let him not eat' (*2 Thess.* 3:10).

The Jews were keenly aware of the divine requirement for honest labour. The Rabbis insisted that every boy should learn a trade. The trade learned by the young Saul of Tarsus was tent-making. Boys were advised 'not to forsake the trade of their fathers'. The Lord Jesus as a lad trained to be a carpenter under the watchful eye of Joseph.

But what God has ordained, Satan opposes. In commercial and financial circles, and often at the highest level, we

[7] E. K. Simpson, *Commentary on the Epistle to the Ephesians* (London: Marshall, Morgan & Scott, 1957), p. 109.

hear of dishonesty and corruption. Shoddy workmanship is not uncommon and amounts to stealing, as does time-wasting and deception on the part of labourers.

The desire for wealth without working for it is another one of Satan's snares. Gambling, endorsed and promoted by governments, is theft. E. K. Simpson states that 'by far the worse purloiner [thief] is the gambler who picks another man's pocket (or else his own) under the cover of a game of chance. Let him that has stolen in this genteel fashion steal no more a march on his neighbour.'[8] It is deplorable that a number of charities resort to 'draws' and 'ballots' to augment their funds. This is pandering to and capitalizing on a prevalent evil. It certainly does nothing to discourage it.

Since the Industrial Revolution, unemployment has been all too common. Thousands can be made redundant at a moment's notice. In many countries the State provided financial assistance in such circumstances. But the unemployed should be constantly on the lookout for fresh employment. State aid, though beneficial, should never be seen as a cushion upon which the remainder of one's life should rest.

In the spiritual realm sloth is equally sinful. Regeneration is the sovereign action of the Holy Spirit and faith is 'the gift of God'. But we have a crucial role to fulfil in the pursuit of holiness.

When it is said that man takes part in the work of sanctification, this does not mean that man is an independent

---

[8] Ibid, p.109 f.

agent in the work, so as to make it partly the work of God and partly the work of man; but merely, that God effects the work in part through the instrumentality of man as a rational being, by requiring of him prayerful and intelligent co-operation with the Spirit.

Louis Berkhof[9]

So in Scripture we are frequently warned against the pitfalls of life (*Rom.*12:9, 16, 17) and exhorted to holy living: 'Work out your own salvation in fear and trembling, for it is God who works in you, both to will and to work for his good pleasure' (*Phil.* 2:12-13).

The believer is called to self-activity, to the active pursuit of the will of God, to the promotion of the spiritual life in himself, to the realization of the virtues of the Christian life, and to a personal application of salvation. He must 'work out' what God in his grace has 'worked in'.

Jac J. Müller[10]

The lackadaisical attitude that permits someone to say 'I am saved', but blinds them to see that conversion is the beginning of a spiritual journey, is ethically and morally disastrous. Often closely linked to what theologians call 'Antinomianism' (*anti* – against, *nomos* – the law), it results from a misunderstanding of Romans 6:14, 'You are not under law but under grace.' These words are mistakenly taken to mean that the law of God is abrogated and its demands no longer apply. This thinking sometimes

[9] Louis Berkhof, *Systematic Theology*, p. 534.
[10] Jac J. Müller, *Epistle of Paul to the Philippians* (London: Marshall, Morgan & Scott, 1955), p. 91.

flows from a failure to see the difference between being under the condemnation of the law, and, when regenerated, lovingly keeping the commandments of our God and gracious heavenly Father. It is also taught by some that the sins of 'the old man' are not accounted to 'the new man'. The appeal to Ephesians 4:22–24, where the terms 'old man' and 'new man' are used, completely misses the point. The apostle is stating that the Christian has entered a totally new way of life, which entails a wholehearted repudiation of all that was wrong in the past. The idea that when a believer does well he does so as the new man and that when he sins he is acting as the old man, is ably refuted by John Murray. The old man has been 'crucified' with Christ (*Rom.* 6:6) and that

> indicates that the old man has been put to death just as decisively as Christ died upon the accursed tree. To suppose that the old man has been crucified and still lives or has been raised again from this death is to contradict the obvious force of the import of crucifixion. And to interject the idea that crucifixion is a slow death and therefore to be conceived of as a process by which the old man is progressively mortified until he is finally put to death is to go flatly counter to Paul's 'crucified', and not 'our old man is in the process of being crucified'.[11]

We must ever remember that 'if anyone is in Christ, he is a new creation. The old has passed away; behold, the new has come' (*2 Cor.* 5:17). Where there is a genuine

[11] John Murray, *Principles of Conduct* (Grand Rapids: Wm. B. Eerdmans, 1957) p. 212 f.

work of the Holy Spirit, this radical change will be apparent.

PROVISION AND HUMAN AGENCY

God's providence often uses human agents to provide for the needy, the sick, and the destitute. Scripture makes frequent reference to this ministry.

> Is not this the fast that I choose, to loose the bonds of wickedness, and undo the straps of the yoke, to let the oppressed go free, and to break every yoke? Is it not to share your bread with the hungry and bring the home-less poor into your house; when you see the naked to cover him, and not to hide yourself from your own flesh? (*Isa.* 58:6–7).

Commenting on this passage, Alec Motyer says, 'It is possible to be socially sensitive and domestically short-sighted.'[12] Ezekiel 18:7,16 strikes the same note. The book of Proverbs contains the warning, 'Whoever closes his ear to the cry of the poor will himself call out and not be answered' (*Prov.* 21:13). Where there is no feeling heart, there will be no helping hand. This sin of omission stems from a hard heart. Then in Proverbs 19:17 we have the striking statement, 'Whoever is generous to the poor lends to the LORD, and he will repay him for his deed.' Explaining this verse, Charles Bridges makes the com-ment, 'The Lord of heaven condescends to be the Surety for the poor. He takes the debt upon himself, and gives us

[12] Alec Motyer, *The Prophecy of Isaiah* (Leicester: Inter-Varsity Press, 1993), p. 481.

the bond of his word in promise of payment.' But Bridges also adds by way of caution that 'it is possible to "give all our goods to feed the poor", without one atom of the true charity of the heart (*1 Cor.* 13:3).'[13]

The New Testament is equally emphatic in stressing and illustrating the duty of caring for the needy. The ministry of Dorcas (*Acts* 9) and the parable of 'the good Samaritan' (*Luke* 10) immediately come to mind. We also have forceful exhortations. In James's practical letter, the apostle asks:

> What good is it, my brothers, if someone says he has faith but does not have works? Can that faith save him? If a brother or sister is poorly clothed and lacking in daily food, and one of you says to them, 'Go in peace, be warmed and filled', without giving them the things needed for the body, what good is that? (*James* 2:14–16).

A similar picture of such heartless conduct is painted in 1 John 3:17–18:

> But if anyone has the world's goods and sees his brother in need, yet closes his heart against him, how does God's love abide in him? Little children, let us not love in word or talk but in deed and in truth.

Such a heartless man as John describes clearly lacks the love of God. Without love and compassion, giving becomes formal, even niggardly.

In this connection it is important to consider the diaconal role of the church. Calvin and the Genevan Reformers

[13] Charles Bridges, *An Exposition of Proverbs* (London: Banner of Truth, 1968) p. 321. Spurgeon called this 'the best book on Proverbs'. A devotional gem.

believed, that while every Christian should show kindness to the needy, the official expression of the church's compassion was through the diaconate. They came to this conclusion on the assumption that the seven men chosen to minister to the needs of certain Greek widows (*Acts* 6) were the first deacons, or at least their forerunners. Certainly the qualifications of the seven match, in large measure, those later required for deacons (*1 Tim.* 3:8–13). The view of the diaconate that Calvin strongly advocated has remained the Reformed view of this office, although in some church circles deacons are often *de facto* elders. In pursuance of his belief, Calvin founded the *Bourse Française*, a fund to assist refugees fleeing from persecution in France. There was also a well organized programme to assist those in need of food, clothing, and medicine.

Jeannine E. Olson gives the following well-documented account of the practical help provided by the *Bourse:*

> The expenditures of the poor ranged in duration from the overnight *viaticum* [costs] given to travellers to lifelong welfare support. Lifelong support was granted to people who were unable to fend for themselves because they were sick, disabled, or aged. Between these two extremes there was a wide range from partial to full support for long or short periods of time to widows, orphans, unemployed able-bodied men, and families who were unable to meet all their expenses. According to need, the deacons provided a weekly handout, clothes, firewood, a Bible or Psalter, a place to stay, a mattress, bedclothes, and occasionally an allotment of grain. They apparently did not

provide ready-made bread until late in the seventeenth century when the deacons arranged with the city hospital to use their ovens. Besides meeting these needs of daily subsistence, the *Bourse* also met extremities by providing medical care, drugs, guardians for the sick, hospitalization, wet nurses for infants, and foster homes for older orphans. To teach people to read and provide them with a trade, the deacons paid school and apprenticeship fees.[14]

The benefits of the diaconal service of the church is not limited to Christians. Worldwide need of whatever kind should always call forth the loving response of the people of God.

Yet in considering this responsibility of the church, several extremes need to be avoided. The 'social gospel' of the liberals and 'liberation theology' so popular in South America, although well-intentioned, seem to forget that the Saviour said, 'Man shall not live by bread alone, but by every word that comes from the mouth of God' (*Matt.* 4:4). Man's first and greatest need is salvation from sin. That does not mean that we will be unconcerned when we see people being oppressed, exploited, or governed by corrupt and dictatorial rulers.

Churches across the globe should expose and condemn such evil in the strongest terms. Confronted by appalling social injustice, and under the guidance of the Holy Spirit, Amos cried, 'Let justice roll down like waters, and righteousness like an ever-flowing stream' (*Amos* 5:24). May

---

[14] Jeannine E. Olson, *Calvin and Social Welfare* (London: Associated University Presses, 1989), p. 179.

we all say 'Amen' to that prayer. But a merely social and horizontal approach does not touch the real heart of humanity's problem.

Christ's word is supremely relevant:

> The Spirit of the Lord GOD is upon me, because the LORD has anointed me to bring good news to the poor, he has sent me to bind up the broken-hearted, to proclaim liberty to the captives, and the opening of the prison to those who are bound; to proclaim the year of the LORD's favour, and the day of vengeance of our God, to comfort all who mourn (*Isa.* 61:1-2; cf. *Luke* 4:18).

Any 'gospel' or theology that falls short of this Christ-centred message is counterfeit. It should be noted that the anointed Conqueror does not hesitate in thought and speech to associate his mission of mercy with the coming day when he will execute the judgment committed to him (*John* 5:22–29).

The existence of state aid does not in the least exempt the church from its corporate duty of caring for the needy. There are many needs that the state does not and cannot meet. The lonely may be visited, the aged transported to and from worship, the blind be read a good book once or twice a week, practical assistance with shopping, grass cutting etc.

The list is endless. All should be done in Christian love. 'Faith apart from works is dead' (*James* 2:26). When body and soul are separated, death results; so 'faith' separated from works is dead (*James* 2:17).

PROVISION AND LIFESTYLE

The present-day search for wealth, grandeur, and pleasure seems insatiable: the more imposing, the more luxurious, the more congenial and gratifying the better! That, in a word, is materialism. God does provide wealth to some by 'lawful' means. But sinful man sees all wealth as his by right. Yet God's word to Israel was clear:

> Beware lest you say in your heart, 'My power and the might of my hand have gained me this wealth.' You shall remember the LORD your God, for it is he who gives you power to get wealth ' (*Deut.* 8:17–18).

There is absolutely no security in godless materialism. Through Amos God said, 'I will strike the winter house along with the summer house, and the houses of ivory shall perish, and the great houses shall come to an end (*Amos* 3:15). In a day when many require a second home, while millions remain homeless, those words should be kept in mind. A day of judgment is assuredly approaching, and of the godless on that day God says, 'Neither their silver nor their gold shall be able to deliver them' (*Zeph.* 1:18).

The contrast, in terms of wealth, between the northern and southern hemispheres is striking. It has been estimated that in the 'Third World' one billion people live on less than one dollar a day, and at best have just a single meal a day! In contrast to the prosperity in so much of the northern hemisphere, we see the distinction between *subsistence* and *luxury*. Even non-Christian writers are pleading for a more frugal lifestyle.

So where does the Christian stand in such a world? Too often we see him setting his heart on earthly possessions. J. B. Phillips translates Matthew 6:24, 'You cannot serve God and the power of money at the same time.' When God gives wealth, there is always the accompanying responsibility of stewardship, how to use that wealth to the glory of God. Some will remind us that 'God. . . richly provides us with everything to enjoy' (*1 Tim.* 6:17); but that is no excuse for extravagance. Many Christians give their tithe, one tenth of their income, to God's work. If done out of love for God, that is good: if done to salve their conscience, that is Pharisaical.

It is possible to combine comfort with a modest lifestyle. The 'health and wealth gospel', popular in some circles, results from a serious misinterpretation of Scripture; it is also foreign to the teaching of Christ, and panders unashamedly to man's covetousness. The Christian should pray, 'Give me neither poverty nor riches; feed me with the food that is needful for me', *i.e.* suitable for my need (*Prov.* 3:8). Where is the Christian's witness if his lifestyle is akin to that of the grasping worldling?

4

THE HAND THAT REDEEMS

One day, Amy Carmichael, the founder and leader of the Dohnavur Fellowship in India, was reading aloud the account of Christ's prayer in Gethsemane: 'My Father, if it be possible, let this cup pass from me; nevertheless, not as I will, but as you will' (*Matt.* 26:39). Arulai, a young girl who was present at the reading, asked, 'What is this cup?' In reply someone suggested that it was 'the suffering of the cross'. 'Oh, no!' she said, 'it could not be that, for I read that when he was going to be crucified, he saw some women crying, and said to them, "Don't cry about me. Cry about yourselves." I don't think it was the cross he minded so much. That could not have been the cup. What was it?' Amy suggested that they should read on and look for further light on this subject. A little later, when she read Christ's cry on the cross, 'My God! My God! Why have you forsaken me?', Arulai was deeply moved and said, 'So the holy God could not look at him. He turned away! He left him all alone! Oh! *that* was the cup.' For the moment it was all too much for her. In telling this story, Amy Carmichael asks, 'How can we get accustomed to the story of such love?'[1]

[1] Amy Carmichael, *Fragments that Remain* (London: SPCK, 1987), p. 100-1.

Arulai had glimpsed the utter darkness, the appalling abandonment of Christ on the cross, when the Father 'could not look at him'. That moment was simultaneously the blackest and the brightest moment of Christ's redemptive suffering; blackest in the sense of utter desertion, brightest because that was the moment when redemption was accomplished. No one can fathom the mystery of this dread cry, but for our sake God 'made him to be sin who knew no sin, so that in him we might become the righteousness of God' (2 *Cor.* 5:21). God made the Sinless One sin for us. Paul does not say that God made him a sinner. Nevertheless, God made the sin-bearer the object of his wrath. In Christ our sins are judged and taken away. It was 'for our sake' that Christ was 'made sin' (*Isa.* 53:5).

Those who regard as reprehensible the idea that Christ on the cross endured the unmitigated wrath of God against sin, and was punished as he stood in our place, have never glimpsed the surpassing holiness of God, the enormity and vileness of sin, and God's total animosity towards it. God's wrath is his holiness in relation to sin. Nor have such objectors seen the wonder of God's love in that he 'did not spare his own Son but gave him up for us all' (*Rom.* 8:32).

> The Father did not spare his own Son. Sparing refers to suffering inflicted. Parents spare their children when they do not inflict the full measure of the chastisement due. Judges spare criminals when they do not pronounce a sentence commensurate with the crime committed. By way of contrast, this is not what the Father did. He did not withhold or lighten one whit of the full toll of judgment

executed upon his own well-beloved and only-begotten Son. There was no alleviation of the stroke . . . There was no mitigation; judgment was dispensed upon the Son in its unrelieved intensity.[2]

Liberal theologians and preachers, who tend to have a low view of God and sin, proclaim a truncated gospel that does not really recognize the righteousness, the justice, and the love of God, which at the cross are displayed in all their fullness and grandeur. At Calvary 'God so loved . . .' (*John* 3:16). 'God so loved . . . that he gave'. He gave that which was most dear to him, 'his only Son'. Redemption comes from the loving heart of God, as Leon Morris says, 'It is not something wrung from him.'[3]

Some verses written in the nineteenth century by William Walsham How put it very simply:

> It is a thing most wonderful,
> Almost too wonderful to be,
> That God's own Son should come from heaven
> And die to save a child like me.

> And yet I know that it is true;
> He came to this poor world below,
> And wept and toiled and mourned and died,
> Only because He loved us so.

It is important to grasp the meaning of the biblical terms 'redeem' and 'redemption'. The religious significance of 'redemption' is drawn from the Old Testament

[2] John Murray, *Romans*, vol. 1, p. 323.
[3] Leon Morris, *John*, p. 229.

where we see God graciously delivering his people from bondage. Israel's deliverance from Egypt was celebrated at the Passover, a festive meal which also prefigured a greater release from the bondage of sin. A Hebrew slave could also be 'redeemed' by the payment of a ransom price (*Lev.* 25:47–55).

So the concept of paying a 'ransom' is associated with 'redemption'. On the cross, Christ paid the ransom for our release from bondage (*Tit.* 2:14; *1 Pet.* 1:18). He came 'to give his life as a ransom for many' (*Matt.* 20:28). The New Testament word 'ransom' (*lutron*) originally referred to the price paid for the release of a prisoner of war. Christ is the great Deliverer. In him we are 'free indeed' (*John* 8:36).

The message proclaimed today from many pulpits and in broadcast talks is one of self-redemption. We are all said to be children of God, innately good and able to live as Jesus lived. In following him, we are said to realize the potential of our own humanity. The cross is seen as a powerful moral influence on mankind, softening human hearts, but not as an expiation for sin nor a satisfaction of divine justice.

That message is as impotent as it is unscriptural. There are those who reject the whole idea of redemption. Albert Einstein wrote: 'There lies before us, if we choose, continual progress in happiness, knowledge and wisdom. Remember your humanity, and forget the rest. If you can do so, the way lies open to a new Paradise.'[4]

---

[4] Quoted by Carl F. H. Henry, *op.cit.*, vol. 4, p. 597.

REDEMPTION ACCOMPLISHED

The consistent message of Scripture is that redemption was accomplished by the substitutionary death of Christ. Isaiah 53, fulfilled in Christ according to the New Testament (*Acts* 8:30–35), allows of no other interpretation. The idea of substitution was central in the Old Testament's sacrificial system. When an Israelite offered a sacrifice to the Lord, he had to lay his hand on the animal's head, confessing his sin as he did so (*Lev.* 1:4). That action symbolized the transference of sin to the offering, and prefigured the one effective sacrifice for sin at Calvary. So the concept of substitution was not new to believing Jews in New Testament times. There are a number of passages in the New Testament where vicarious or substitutionary atonement is expressly stated. 'Christ redeemed us from the curse of the law by becoming a curse for us (*Gal.* 3:13). 'Christ, having been offered once to bear the sin of many will appear a second time, not to deal with sin but to save those who are eagerly waiting for him' (*Heb.* 9:28). 'He himself bore our sins in his body on the tree, that we might die to sin and live to righteousness' (*1 Pet.* 2:24). The guilt of sin, in terms of liability to punishment, was imputed to Christ, not our actual sinfulness: that would be an utter impossibility and would nullify the entire work of redemption. Just as the sacrificial lamb had to be 'without blemish' (*Exod.* 12:5), so Christ on the cross was 'a lamb without blemish or spot' (*1 Pet.* 1:19).

Some are happy to speak about substitution, but they deny that it was penal in nature. Instead, they see Christ's suffering as a mere sympathetic sharing in our sorrows. Others reject the idea of substitution altogether as an unjust and therefore morally dangerous concept. They say that it is wrong to make the innocent suffer for the wicked. This objection, however, overlooks the fact that the plan of redemption resulted from a solemn agreement between the three Persons of the Godhead, in which the Son *voluntarily* undertook to bear the penalty for the sins of his people. Not only is it true that the Father sent the Son 'to be the Saviour of the world' (*1 John* 4:14), but it is equally true that 'Christ loved the church and gave himself up for her' (*Eph.* 5:25). Paul could speak of 'the Son of God, who loved me and gave himself for me' (*Gal.* 2:20).

Voluntary substitution! If the Father had merely sent the Son into the world to suffer a shameful, pointless death, then such a thing would indeed have been cruel and unjust. Sadly, in recent times, some professed evangelicals have joined the chorus of those who oppose the doctrine of penal substitution, despite the fact that this doctrine is so emphatically taught in Scripture. Once one removes penal substitution from the gospel, there is no 'good news' left to take to sinners.

Christ's death was not some kind of divine experiment that had no assured result. It was not a test undertaken in the vague hope that it might succeed. From all eternity God chose a definite number of mankind for redemption. They were chosen in Christ, for Christ, and given to Christ (*Eph.*1:4; *John* 17:2). They were not a 'chosen few', for in the Revelation given to the apostle John they appeared as 'a great multitude that no one could number, from every nation, from all tribes and peoples and languages' (*Rev.* 7:9). Their salvation was assured when Christ died for their sins. There was no possibility of Christ failing in his mission. So certain was he of victory that he could say to the Father before he went to the cross, 'I glorified you on earth, having accomplished the work that you gave me to do' (*John* 17:4). Again he could say confidently, 'Now is the judgement of this world, now will the ruler of this world be cast out' (*John* 12:31). He was not speaking of ultimate victory, but victory *'now'*.

The redemption of men and women is due solely to God's sovereign election. Fallen man had no claim on God. God could have left all mankind to perish in their sins, and been perfectly just, even as he left the fallen angels to await his wrath (*Jude* 6). The redeemed are debtors to God's sovereign grace. Calvin says:

> In order really to experience this free bounty, we must lay down all ideas of worth or merit, and first look to God's free election, then his calling. Why have our minds been enlightened through the knowledge of the gospel? Have we merited anything? Not at all; God chose us before we were born, indeed even before the creation of the world, as it says in that other passage (*Eph.* 1:4). Here, then, is where we must begin.[5]

This truth goes against the grain of human pride, which must be subdued if we are to know the comfort of this doctrine and praise God for his marvellous salvation.

---

[5] John Calvin, *Sermons on Galatians* (Edinburgh: Banner of Truth, 1997), p. 77, on *Gal.* 1:11–14.

Here we encounter one of the fundamental differences between the theological systems known as Arminianism and Calvinism. It is meaningless to say, as Arminians do, that God foresaw who would believe and chose them on the basis of their foreseen faith: that is no choice at all. One wonders how anyone can read the relevant passages of Scripture and reach such a conclusion. Besides, it is only possible to foreknow a certainty. On what does the certainty of our salvation rest? It is rendered certain by divine predestination. 'In him [Christ] we have obtained an inheritance, having been predestined according to the purpose of him who works all things according to the counsel of his will (*Eph.* 1:11).

According to Arminianism, Christ died to make salvation possible for all, yet certain for none. All is said to hinge on man's decision as he exercises his free will. While the Calvinist maintains that man does act freely, he also understands that free action in terms of man's fallen nature; as one who is 'alienated from the life of God', 'hostile in mind' and God's 'enemy' (*Eph.* 4:18; *Col.* 1:21; *Rom.* 5:10), sinful man, in and of himself, will never come to Christ for life (*John* 5:40). If, as the Arminian maintains, Christ died for the sins of all without exception, then all should be saved. However, we are told that many perish because of unbelief. Yet, unbelief is a sin, and arguably one that lies close to the heart of every sin! In this respect, there is a blind spot in Arminian reasoning.

The Bible makes it abundantly plain that Christ did not come to place all in a salvable state: he came to save those ordained to eternal life (*Matt.* 1:21). He did not come to make men redeemable: he 'obtained eternal, redemption' for his people (*Heb.* 9:12, KJV). Christ accomplished the redemption of the elect. He says 'I have come down from heaven, not to do my own will but the will of him who sent me. And this is the will of him who sent me, that I should lose nothing of all he has given me; but raise it up on the last day' (*John* 6:38–39). There we have the great truth of definite redemption, not some open-ended, unpredictable venture.

It is said that the doctrine of election, as defined in the historic Reformed confessions, fosters spiritual pride and careless living, reduces human beings to robots, gives the unbeliever an excuse for rejecting the gospel offer, and renders the preaching of the gospel unnecessary. As we shall see, none of these arguments is valid: indeed the exact opposite is the case.

REDEMPTION APPLIED

Decreed by the Triune God from all eternity, accomplished by God the Son, redemption is savingly applied to men and women by God the Holy Spirit. He uses the preaching of the Word to call men and women effectually to trust Christ. Effectual calling is defined in the *Westminster Larger Catechism* in this way:

> Effectual calling is the work of God's almighty power and grace, whereby (out of his free and special love to his elect, and from nothing in them moving him thereunto) he doth, in his accepted time, invite and draw them to Jesus Christ by his word and Spirit; savingly

enlightening their minds, renewing and powerfully determining their wills, so as they (although in themselves dead in sin) are hereby made willing and able freely to answer his call, and to accept and embrace the grace offered and conveyed therein. (Answer 67)

It is imperative that the gospel is preached to all, as this is the means God uses to draw his elect people to the Saviour. Paul writes, 'Everyone who calls on the name of the Lord will be saved' (*Rom.* 10:13). He then asks: 'But how are they to call on him in whom they have not believed? And how are they to believe in him of whom they have never heard? And how are they to hear without someone preaching?' Then he quotes Isaiah 52:7: 'How beautiful are the feet of those who preach the good news!' (*Rom.* 10:14–15). The apostle who emphasized so strongly the doctrines of predestination and election preached the gospel passionately and tirelessly. He knew that without such preaching men and women would not be saved. Election is God's business; our business is to preach the gospel and leave the results in God's hand.

The Holy Spirit makes the preached Word effective when he regenerates the soul (*John* 3:3, 5–8), grants faith and repentance (*Eph.* 2:8; *Acts* 5:31), and sanctifies the believer (*Rom.* 15:16; 2 *Thess.* 2:13). 'No one can say "Jesus is Lord" except in the Holy Spirit (*1 Cor.* 12:3), and 'Anyone who does not have the Spirit of Christ does not belong to him' (*Rom.* 8:9).

We are said to be 'born of the Spirit' (*John* 3:6). This spiritual birth is supernatural in character. Having spoken to Nicodemus about the necessity of the new birth in order to see and enter the kingdom of God, the Saviour said: 'The wind blows where it wishes, and you hear its sound, but you do not know where it comes from or where it goes. So it is with everyone who is born of the Spirit (*John* 3:8). Believers are 'born'. As in natural birth so in the new birth, we do not decide to give ourselves birth. We did not and cannot decide to be 'born again'. The Saviour's words to Nicodemus about the new birth are not a command but a plain statement of fact. John Murray observes that

> We do not have spiritual perception of the kingdom of God nor do we enter into it because we willed to or decided to. If the privilege is ours it is because the Holy Spirit willed it and here all rests upon the Holy Spirit's decision and action.

Referring to John 3:8, Murray adds

> The wind is not at our beck and call; neither is the regenerative operation of the Spirit . . . the Spirit's work is mysterious. All points up the sovereignty, efficacy, and inscrutability of the Holy Spirit's work in regeneration.[6]

From the moment of the new birth until our redemption is complete in glory, the role of the Holy Spirit is central and crucial. By him we are 'sealed for the day of redemption' (*Eph.* 4:30). The seal is the mark of ownership. By the Spirit, God stamps the redeemed as his own possession, and the Holy Spirit is that seal.

---

[6] John Murray, *Redemption: Accomplished and Applied* (London: Banner of Truth, 1961), p. 99.

The truth of God's sovereign election of his people, and their sovereign renewal by the Holy Spirit, in no way detract from human responsibility: 'God . . . commands all people everywhere to repent' (*Acts* 17:30). It is a sin to disobey this command and we are responsible to God if we fail to obey. The sovereignty of God and human responsibility appear to our finite minds as parallel lines that never meet. Both are emphasized throughout the Bible. When Spurgeon was asked how to reconcile these twin truths, he answered that he was commanded to preach them, not to reconcile them! Besides, he added, they are friends and therefore do not stand in need of reconciliation.

In this life, at least, we shall struggle with unanswered questions, but it is not necessary to be fully conversant with every Christian doctrine in order to be a Christian. A young child may be enabled by the Holy Spirit to trust the Lord Jesus. He may know little or nothing of predestination and election: he does not need to, not yet. The penitent criminal on the cross who trusted in Christ, knew nothing of predestination and election: he did not need to. The present writer watched an old man on his deathbed look to Christ and find peace. He knew nothing of predestination and election: he did not need to. The maturing Christian, however, should 'grow in the knowledge and grace of Christ', progressing from 'milk' to 'solid food'. In the epistle to the Hebrews we read that 'everyone who lives on milk is unskilled in the word of righteousness, since he is a child. But solid food is for the mature' (*Heb.* 5:13–14). Milk is suitable and appropriate for babies, but new born souls are not meant to remain spiritual infants for ever.

J. C. Ryle has a beautiful and well-applied illustration of this very point, which is worth quoting in full.

The plain truth is that God's scheme of salvation is like a ladder let down from heaven to earth, to bring together the holy God, and the sinful creature, man. God is at the top of the ladder and man is at the bottom. The top of the ladder is far above, out of sight, and we have no eyes to see it. There, at the top of that ladder, are God's eternal purposes, – His everlasting covenant, His election, His predestination of a people to be saved by Christ. From the top of the ladder comes down that full and rich provision of mercy for sinners which is revealed to us in the Gospel. The bottom of that ladder is close to sinful man on earth, and consists of the simple steps of repentance and faith. By them he must begin to climb upwards. In the humble use of them he shall mount higher and higher every year, and get clearer glimpses of good things yet to come. What can be more plain than the duty of using the steps which are close to our hands? What can be more foolish than to say, I will not put my foot on the steps at the bottom, until I clearly under-stand the steps at the top? . . . Jesus Christ stands before us, saying, 'Come unto Me!' Let us not waste time doubting, quibbling, and disputing. Let us come to Christ at once, just as we are. Let us lay hold and believe![7]

[7] J. C. Ryle, *Old Paths* (Edinburgh: Banner of Truth, 1999), p. 473–4.

Once we, 'lay hold and believe', the Spirit of God will lead us 'into all the truth' (*John* 16:13). The illustration is sometimes used in which entrance to the kingdom is likened to a gateway. Above the gate are the words, 'Whoever comes to me I will never cast out.' Entering and looking back one can see on the inside of the gate the words, 'All that the Father gives me will come to me' (*John* 6:37). Christ stands by his promise that if we come to him he will never refuse us. Anyone who wants to be saved may be saved, provided that person believes and obeys the gospel: God's way of salvation is the only way.

It is a source of great comfort for the believer to consider what has been termed 'the golden chain' of Romans 8:29–30:

> For those whom he foreknew[8] he also predestined . . . and those whom he predestined he also called, and those whom he called he also justified and those whom he justified he also glorified.

The same number chosen from all eternity will without exception be glorified. There is not a weak link in this chain. Definite redemption!

In spite of the wonderfully comforting teaching of Romans 8 there are Christians who sincerely believe that a true believer may fall totally and finally from grace and perish eternally. In support of this view, appeal is made to

---

[8] B. B. Warfield refers here to 'the pregnant use of "know"', likening it to Amos 3:2, 'You only have I known out of all the families of the earth.' B. B. Warfield, *Selected Shorter Writings* (Nutley: Presbyterians and Reformed Publishing Co. 1970), vol. 1, p. 290.

the apostasy passages in the epistles to the Hebrews. For example in Hebrews 6:4–6 we read that

> it is impossible to restore again to repentance those who have once been enlightened, who have tasted the heavenly gift and have shared in the Holy Spirit, and have tasted the goodness of the word of God and the power of the age to come, if they then fall away, since they are crucifying once again the Son of God to their own harm and holding him up to contempt.

Bearing in mind that God's Word does not contradict itself, it is helpful to consider such passages in the light of our Lord's parable of the sower (*Mark* 4:1–20). The Lord himself has supplied us with an infallible interpretation of this parable. At first sight, the results following the sowing of the seed are impressive. Church statisticians, who like to focus on figures, percentages, and graphs, would have been elated by these results. Yet only one of the four sowings of the seed (the seed that fell into the good soil), was really effective.

Philip E. Hughes comments helpfully:

> It is not enough to have the name of the Lord on one's lips in worship and invocation. Even to prophesy and to cast out demons and to do mighty works in the Lord's name does not necessarily guarantee trueness of heart (*Matt.* 7:21–23; 25:11 f.) . . . The sin of apostasy, then, is a grim (and far more than a merely hypothetical) possibility for persons who through identification with the people of God have been brought within the sphere of divine blessing. They may be baptized, as Simon Magus

was, occupied in Christian labours, as Demas was, endowed with charismatic gifts, preachers even, healers of the sick and casters out of demons, and privileged to belong to an inner circle of disciples, as Judas was (*Mark* 6:12 f.; *Matt.*10:5 ff.), and yet their heart may be far from the One they profess to serve.[9]

It is a sobering thought that in religious terms there are no hypocrites outside the church. Atheists and agnostics are what they profess to be. Perseverance is one of the marks of a truly regenerate person. John, in his First Letter writes. 'They went out from us, but they were not of us, for if they had been of us, they would have continued with us. But they went out, that it might become plain that they all are not of us' (*1 John* 2:19). The writer to the Hebrews, who gives these solemn warnings about the danger of apostasy, also states: 'But we are not of those who shrink back and are destroyed, but of those who have faith and preserve their souls' (*Heb.* 10:39). God 'gave his only Son, that whoever believes in him should not perish but have eternal life' (*John* 3:16).

Noah fell into drunkenness. Abraham lied twice about his wife Sarah, saying she was his sister and thus risking her honour to save his own skin. Lot chose Sodom, Jacob cheated his brother Esau and deceived his father Isaac. David committed adultery with Bathsheba and then tried to cover it up by having her husband, Uriah, killed. In Gethsemane the disciples abandoned Jesus to

[9] Philip E. Hughes, *Commentary on the Epistle to the Hebrews* (Grand Rapids: Wm. B. Eerdmans, 1977), p. 217 f.

protect their own lives. Paul and Barnabas fought over John Mark and had to part company. Paul persisted in returning to Jerusalem with the offering from the Gentiles when even the Lord himself appeared to him and forbade him to do it. All these sinned. Yet they were not lost. In fact, there is not a single story in the whole Bible of one who was truly a child of God who was lost. Many were overtaken by sin, but none perished.[10]

There have, of course, been Christians of Arminian persuasion, who have displayed an earnest passion for lost souls and who have in many ways lived an exemplary life. God not only used the Calvinist George Whitefield, but also the Arminian John Wesley in the gathering of many thousands of souls into the kingdom during the Great Awakening of the eighteenth century. While this fact is important to recognize, we ought not to allow our doctrinal convictions to rest upon the teachings of a preacher or theologian, no matter how blest their ministries were by God. The Bible is our *only* rule of faith (what we are to believe) and life (how we are to live). We must follow the example of the Bereans of old, who when they heard Paul and Silas preach, examined 'the Scriptures daily to see if these things were so' (*Acts* 17:11). The Scriptures alone are to determine the soundness of our doctrine.

When Christians pray, they ask God to save this person or that person, to restore a backslider, to heal a sick person, and to revive the church. Why do they do so? It is because they believe that God is sovereign and is able to

[10] James Montgomery Boice, *Foundations of the Christian Faith* (Downers Grove: InterVarsity Press, 1986), p. 520.

answer their prayers according to his will. At the throne of grace all Christians are of one mind and humbly bow before the King.

REDEMPTION CONFIRMED

When our sins were laid on the Lord Jesus, his righteousness was credited to us. God sees us clothed in the righteousness of his Son and declares us to be righteous. This declaration of God regarding the believing sinner is known as justification. Justification does not make us righteous. It is an act of God's free grace that results in the radical reversal of our standing before God. Our standing before God has been altered for ever. The guilt of our sin has been removed and we are now forgiven. 'Who shall bring any charge against God's elect? It is God who justifies' (*Rom.* 8:33; cf. *Rom.* 3:26). The Bible teaches that we are justified by faith (*Rom.* 5:1). Faith is the instrument by which we experience justification. The New Testament makes it clear that we are justified by faith *alone*. 'For we hold that one is justified by faith apart from the works of the law' (*Rom.* 3:28, cf. 5:1; *Gal.* 3:16; 3:24). Although we are justified by faith alone, that faith is *never alone,* but is always accompanied by a changed life. In this way redemption is confirmed in our experience and we know that we are among the number of God's elect.

The Bible exhorts us to make our 'calling and election sure' (2 *Pet.* 1:10). Alexander Nisbet observed that 'this jewel of assurance does not fall in the lap of any lazy soul, nor can any expect to attain to it . . . in whose hearts grace is without exercise, and whose conversation [way of life] is without fruitfulness.'[11] As stated in Ephesians 2:9–10, we are not saved *by* good works, but *for* good works. God chose us in Christ 'before the foundation of the world, that we should be holy and blameless before him' (*Eph.* 1:4). God chose us to be holy. Therefore, we cannot be assured of our election without holiness of life. Holiness is not hallowed mystical feeling, but a grateful and loving obedience to our Lord's commands. No one has the right to regard himself as one of God's elect who does not actually live the Christian life. Christ said, 'If you abide in my word, you are truly my disciples' (*John* 8:31).

The *Westminster Confession of Faith* speaks of 'an infallible assurance of faith', and says: 'This infallible assurance doth not so belong to the essence of faith, but that a true believer may wait long, and conflict with many difficulties before he be a partaker of it.' It then states that the believer may 'in the right use of ordinary means, attain thereunto' (VIII:2, 3). 'Ordinary means' here refers to the Bible read and preached, prayer, baptism and the Lord's Supper, worship, and Christian fellowship. This section of the *Confession* concludes with the reminder that assurance of salvation may be 'shaken' and 'diminished' by negligence, falling into sin, or by God 'withdrawing the light of his countenance'. Yet believers are

> never utterly destitute of the seed of God, and life of faith, that love of Christ and the brethren, that sincerity of heart, and conscience of duty, out of which, by the operation of the Spirit, this assurance may, in due time, be

[11] Alexander Nisbet, *An Exposition of 1 and 2 Peter* (Edinburgh: Banner of Truth Trust, 1982), p. 231.

revived; and by the which, in the mean time, they are supported from utter despair' (VIII:4).

It should be noted that the *Confession* does *not* say that assurance does not belong to the essence of faith, but that it 'doth not so *belong* . . . but that a true believer may wait long . . . before he be a partaker of it.' However it is the Christian's duty to be '*diligent*' to make his 'calling and election sure' (*1 Pet.*1:10). Near the end of the First Epistle of John we read, 'I write these things to you who believe in the name of the Son of God that you may know that you have eternal life' (*1 John* 5:13). And again, 'And by this we know that we have come to know him, if we keep his commandments' (2:3). 'The Spirit himself bears witness with our spirit that we are children of God' (*Rom.* 8:15).

When someone is 'born of the Spirit', he repents of his sin and trusts in Christ alone for salvation. How often, or perhaps how seldom, is repentance emphasized in pulpits today? Yet it was a dominant note in apostolic preaching, indeed in the whole of the Bible.

The person who is reconciled to God through the cross of Christ is also adopted into the family of God. So Paul could write: 'And because you are sons, God has sent the Spirit of his Son into our hearts, crying, "Abba! Father!"'

Like justification, adoption is an act of God's grace. It alters our standing before God but does not change our character. That process of change, our growth in grace (sanctification) is the on-going work of the Holy Spirit. In this way we develop the family likeness as the children of God. Effectual calling, regeneration, justification and adoption are all included in the term 'salvation'.

It is important to avoid the error of hyper-Calvinism, which fails to do justice to the Bible's emphasis on human responsibility. Paul wrote to the Corinthians: 'We implore you on behalf of Christ, be reconciled to God' (2 *Cor.* 5:20). Through the prophet Ezekiel God appealed to sinful Israel, saying: 'Turn back, turn back from your evil ways, for why will you die, O house of Israel?' (*Ezek.* 33:11). Matthew Henry, commenting upon this verse says, 'It is certain that God is sincere and in earnest in the calls he gives to repent . . .To repent is to turn from our evil way; this God requires sinners to do; this he urges them to do by repeated instances . . . O that they would be prevailed with to turn, to turn quickly, without delay!' We need with burning hearts to entreat and beseech sinners to repent and obey the gospel. Cold, theoretical preaching does not come from a heart aflame for God; a preacher who lacks passion will not touch the hearts of his hearers.

There is nothing in human experience more radical, more dynamic, more comprehensive and more life changing than conversion. But conversion is only the beginning of a walk with God – a walk that will transform every aspect of our lives. In Psalm 90:17 we have the prayer: 'And let the beauty of the LORD our God be upon us' (KJV). It is wonderful when we see that beauty reflected in the godly life and character of the Christian. The poet Tennyson said of Archbishop Trench that it was impossible to look upon him and not love him. Oh that there were more Christians like that! Courageous when courage is needed, but at all times loving, tender-hearted, and Christlike. The witness of such Christians would make a powerful impact for the gospel in this cold and harsh world!

5

THE HAND THAT KEEPS

When Geoffrey Bull, missionary to China, was arrested by the Communists and imprisoned, he did not know that three years of incarceration lay before him. Later he wrote, 'So I settled down fairly comfortably to my first night as a captive in the hands of the Communists and yet, in the most real sense, in the hands of the Lord. In his infinite grace he shielded from my eyes the fact that more than another eleven hundred and fifty evenings would yet pass before I slept again in freedom.' During those years he was to receive merciless treatment. Yet amid his fears and mental struggles, he never forgot that he was in God's hands. He recalled some lines penned by Amy Carmichael:

> '*And a light shined in the cell*'
> And there was not any wall
> And there was no dark at all
> Only Thou, Immanuel.
>
> Light of Love shined in the cell
> Turned to gold the iron bars,
> Opened windows to the stars,
> Peace stood there as sentinel.[1]

[1] Geoffrey T. Bull, *When Iron Gates Yield* (London: Hodder & Stoughton, 1955), pp. 123, 192.

When Samuel Rutherford was consigned to house-arrest in Aberdeen, he said, 'I go to my King's palace at Aberdeen; tongue, pen, and wit cannot express my joy.'[2] At a time of danger, King David could write: 'My times are in your hand, rescue me from the hand of my enemies and persecutors! (*Psa.* 31:15). He was aware of two hands, one was that of his enemies and the other that of his God. The reality of God's sovereignty brought him peace, as it has done so often for the people of God when they have found themselves in times of adversity and distress.

THE HAND THAT KEEPS US PROM FALLING

Viewing the earthly prosperity of the wicked together with their pride and arrogance, the Psalmist confessed, 'But as for me, my feet had almost stumbled, my steps had nearly slipped' (*Psa.* 73:2). Almost! – It was only as he bowed in worship before the Lord that he saw things from a different perspective. It was in 'the sanctuary' that he 'discerned their end' (*Psa.* 73:17). It was then that he received assurance and was able to say to God: 'Nevertheless, I am continually with you; you hold my right hand' (*Psa.* 73:23). Calvin comments here:

> When the Psalmist speaks of God as *holding him by the right hand,* he means that he was, by the wonderful power of God, drawn back from the deep gulf into which the reprobate cast themselves . . . The force of the

---

[2] Alexander Smellie, *Men of the Covenant* (London: Banner of Truth Trust, 1960), p. 67.

metaphor contained in the language, which represented God as *holding us by the right hand*, is to be particularly noticed; for there is no temptation, let it be ever so slight, which would not easily overthrow us, were we not upheld and sustained by the power of God.[3]

The thought of God holding his people by his hand recurs throughout the Bible: 'All his holy ones were in his hand' (*Deut.* 33:3); 'My soul clings to you; your right hand upholds me' (*Psa.* 63:8, cf. *Psa.* 139:9–10). Christians are 'kept by the power of God through faith unto salvation (*1 Pet.* 1:5, KJV). 'Kept by the power of God'! How easily and thoughtlessly we read such wonderful words! The power of God is infinite. It is *that power* that keeps the people of God eternally secure. The Psalmist could say 'when I thought, "My foot slips", your steadfast love, O LORD, held me up' (*Psa.* 94:18). The believer may stumble and fall, but that fall is neither total nor final: 'Though he fall he shall not be cast headlong, for the LORD upholds his hand' (*Psa.* 37.23–24 cf. *Psa.* 56:13; 116:8; 121:3; *Prov.* 3:26). This comforting truth does not allow us to be slack in our Christian walk. We are 'kept by the power of God *through faith*'. John Murray comments:

> Let us not then take refuge in our sloth or encouragement in our lust from the abused doctrine of the security of the believer. But let us appreciate the doctrine of the perseverance of the saints and recognize that we may entertain the faith of our security in Christ only as we

[3] John Calvin, *Psalms*, vol. 3, p. 152.

persevere in faith and holiness to the end . . . The perseverance of the saints reminds us forcefully that only those who persevere to the end are truly saints. We do not attain to the prize of the high calling of God in Christ Jesus automatically. Perseverance means the engagement of our persons in the most intense and concentrated devotion to those means which God has ordained for the achievement of his saving purpose.[4]

'I have been saved several times, but I could never keep it up.' Occasionally the pastor receives such a response when speaking to someone about his or her spiritual state. In an emotional and highly charged atmosphere, a 'decision' had been made, but not in the context of sound biblical teaching. Faith is not a leap in the dark: it is never exercised in a vacuum of knowledge. Those who have been disillusioned as the result of shallow evangelism may yet come to an assurance of salvation if they are lovingly shown the true nature of repentance and faith, and the faithfulness of God. Only then may that person say with Paul: 'I know whom I have believed, and I am convinced that he is able to guard what I have entrusted to him until that day' (2 *Tim.* 1:12, NASB).

THE HAND THAT KEEPS US IN SORROW AND AFFLICTION

In the New Testament, this present age is seen as one of affliction for the church. Believers are depicted as suffering for the sake of the kingdom. To the Philippians Paul

---

[4] John Murray, *Redemption: Accomplished and Applied*, p. 193.

wrote: 'For it has been granted to you that for the sake of Christ you should not only believe in him but also suffer for his sake' (*Phil.* 1:29). To his disciples Christ said, 'In the world you will have tribulation. But take heart, I have overcome the world' (*John* 16:33). Because of Christ's triumph over the world and the certainty of his coming in judgment, 'we rejoice in our sufferings' (*Rom.* 5:3). We have an unshakeable hope that focuses on the 'appearing' of Christ (*Titus* 2:13). In Romans 8:18 we have Paul's stirring affirmation: 'For I consider that the sufferings of this present time are not worth comparing with the glory that is to be revealed to us.' We also recall our Saviour's words: 'Blessed are you when others revile you and persecute you and utter all kinds of evil against you falsely on my account. Rejoice and be glad, for your reward is great in heaven, for so they persecuted the prophets who were before you' (*Matt.* 5:11-12). When the cold winds of hostility blow upon us, what are we to do? 'Rejoice and be glad'! Has any other faith anything to compare with this? What an honour it is to suffer for Christ's sake!

In a more general sense, sorrow and affliction come to all sooner or later. The experience of sorrow can be a time for reflection.

> I walked a mile with Pleasure,
>   She chattered all the way,
> But left me none the wiser,
>   For all she had to say.
>
> I walked a mile with Sorrow,
>   And ne'er a word said she;

> But, oh, the things I learned from her
> When Sorrow walked with me!

Robert Browning Hamilton, *Along the Road*

Sorrow by itself has no liberating message: many are embittered by it. If, however, Christ is with us in our sorrow, and his Word is in our hearts, and we are much in prayer, then all is changed. There is a loving hand to uphold us in times of suffering and loss.

> When as we shall feel the griefs, anguishes, and afflictions of this world . . . let us have recourse unto this word of God: for in it we shall find him to stretch forth his hand to draw us unto him, declaring that he will help the afflicted, have pity on the miserable and vexed, aid the wretched, desireth nothing else but to bring back again poor sinners which will yield themselves unto him, lay all their cares in his lap, and that he will unburden us of them all.[5]

When David was surrounded by enemies and declared, 'I hear the whispering of many – terror on every side! – as they scheme together against me, as they plot to take my life', he could also say, 'But I trust in you, O LORD; I say "You are my God". My times are in your hand' (*Psa.* 31:13–15). That has been the testimony of God's people throughout history.

Sorrow and adversity can strike suddenly and devastatingly. They can plunge us into an abyss of darkness and fear. Christians are not exempt from such trials; they, too,

---

[5] John Calvin, *Sermons on Psalm 119* (Audubon: Old Paths Publications, 1996), p. 368.

may experience disease, bereavement, unemployment, and disappointment. Christians are not insulated from sorrow and suffering. They follow a crucified Saviour and the shadow of Christ's cross is cast upon their path. Besides, if believers were sheltered from pain and grief, how could they witness to God's all-sufficient and sustaining grace? It is precisely in such situations that Christians are to witness to the reality of their faith.

It is important to remember that, while God can and sometimes does heal, we cannot and must not make demands of God when all else fails. We may pray for someone's healing *if it is God's will*. On many occasions it is not his will to heal and, in such cases, he exercises his sovereignty for wise and gracious purposes. The apostle Paul suffered a sore and troublesome affliction, 'a thorn given me in the flesh, a messenger of Satan to harass me, to keep me from being too elated.' He tells the Corinthians: 'Three times I pleaded with the Lord about this, that it should leave me. But he said to me, "My grace is sufficient for you, for my power is made perfect in weakness"' (2 *Cor.* 12:7–9). 'To keep me from being too elated'! There was a merciful purpose behind this affliction, which the sufferer was given to understand. This in itself brought a measure of comfort and Paul was able to add: 'For when I am weak, then am I strong' (2 *Cor.* 12:10). God promised him that divine grace sufficient for his need would be his constant portion.

Philip E. Hughes asks:

Is there a single servant of Christ who cannot point to some 'thorn in the flesh', visible or private, physical or psychological, from which he had prayed to be released, but which has been given him by God to keep him humble, and therefore, fruitful, in his service?[6]

There is nothing more bleak than worldly sorrow. It stands in sharp contrast to the Christian's experience of sorrow. Paul speaks of 'a godly sorrow' that resulted in repentance, and contrasts it with 'the sorrow of the world' that produced death (2 *Cor.* 7:10). The latter sorrow is of the very essence of sin. Instead of leading to repentance, it produces self-pity. It may be bitter and intense like that of Esau who, in spite of his many tears, remained impenitent (*Heb.* 12:16 f.). Whereas the deep sorrow of David expressed itself in repentance as he prayed, 'Wash me thoroughly from my iniquity, and cleanse me from my sin!' (*Psa.* 51:2).

It is true that trial and sorrow may not be related to any particular sin, yet the contrast between the sorrow of the believer and that of the worldling remains. The life that is built on Christ the solid rock will stand when the storm of adversity breaks, whereas the life that rests on the sands of self-centred, humanistic philosophy will fall and its ruin will be great (*Luke* 6:47–49). So it will be at the final judgment.

THE HAND THAT KEEPS US WHEN DEJECTED

Christians can and sometimes do suffer from depression. Clinical depression can result from some deficiency in the body and requires medical help. But, generally, depression

---

[6] Philip E. Hughes, *Paul's Second Epistle to the Corinthians* (London: Marshall, Morgan & Scott, 1962), p. 442 f.

does not belong to that category. Depression can have many causes, health problems, financial insecurity, children who bring disappointment, a difficult relative, bereavement. The pastor of a congregation with a few prickly saints and perhaps an awkward office-bearer, can easily become depressed. In all such cases anti-depressants are not the solution. They simply mask the problem, but do not deal with the cause.

However deep and lasting the depression, the child of God need not finally succumb to it. The Christian poet William Cowper struggled with recurring depression, verging on despair. Once he wrote to his friend John Newton: 'The future appears as gloomy as ever; and I seem to myself to be scrambling always in the dark, among rocks and precipices, without a guide, but with an enemy at my heels, prepared to push me headlong.'[7] It is hard to read Cowper's Christian verse and not be moved:

> The Lord will happiness divine
> On contrite hearts bestow;
> Then tell me, gracious God, is mine
> A contrite heart, or no?

He asks:

> Where is the blessedness I knew
> When first I saw the Lord?

Yet his Christian faith emerged from the gloom, and shone brightly:

---

[7] Quoted by A. E. Pratt in *Biographical Dictionary of Evangelicals* (Leicester: Inter-Varsity Press, 2003), p. 162.

> God is his own interpreter
> And he will make it plain.

Whatever one may think of these lines, they do show Cowper's resurgent Christian faith. Cowper may be an extreme example of despondency, but his experience illustrates the truth that nothing 'will be able to separate us from the love of God in Christ Jesus our Lord' (*Rom.* 8:39). The Psalmist asked, 'Why are you cast down, O my soul, and why are you in turmoil within me?' (*Psa.* 42:5, 11; 43:5) But his faith did not fail: 'Hope in God for I shall again praise him, my salvation and my God.' In Psalm 55:22 we have words of comfort and encouragement: 'Cast your burden on the LORD and he will sustain you, he will never permit the righteous to be moved.' Take your burden to the Lord in prayer; meditate on his Word; cling to Christ and *'he will sustain you'*; 'for all the promises of God find their "Yes" in him' (2 *Cor.* 1:20).

THE HAND THAT KEEPS US IN YOUTH

The book of Proverbs provides much counsel for young people. It contains both words of warning and encouragement. There is warning against fornication (a forgotten word in our modern society, but a prevalent evil) and promiscuous sexual behaviour (*Prov.* 6:23–29), against involvement in criminal gangs (*Prov.* 1:10–19), against drunkenness (*Prov.* 20:1), against deceit (*Prov.* 20:10–11), against sloth (*Prov.* 6:6–11), against falsehood (*Prov.* 6:16–19), against disrespect shown to parents (*Prov.* 15:20). There is encouragement to seek wisdom (*Prov.* 3:13–18), to honour parents (*Prov.* 4:1–4; 10:1), to accept chastisement (*Prov.* 29:15), to see the value and beauty of a godly woman (*Prov.* 31:10–31). In Proverbs the bitter consequences of sinful ways and the blessedness of a godly life are vividly portrayed.

J. C. Ryle prepared an address entitled 'Thoughts for Young Men' (sixty pages in print!), equally suitable for young women. It was forthright and heart-searching. We give several short quotations from it.

> Youth is the seed-time of full age, the moulding season in the little space of human life, the turning-point in the history of man's mind. By the shoot we judge of the tree, by the blossoms we judge of the fruit, by the spring we judge of the harvest, by the morning we judge of the day, and by the character of the young man, we generally judge what he will be when he grows up.[8]

Since this is true, how important it is that children are taught the truths of God's Word. 'Train up a child in the way he should go, even when he is old he will not depart from it' (*Prov.* 22:6). In every age, young people face many temptations and pitfalls, and perhaps never more so than today. It is tragic to see millions of young people swept along in a tide of reckless abandonment to every form of self-indulgence, with all the ensuing spiritual and physical consequences. 'The way of transgressors is hard' or 'ruinous' (*Prov.* 13:15, KJV). We see a generation of young people totally ignorant of God's Word. Watching university students in televised quiz programmes, it is

[8] J. C. Ryle, *The Upper Room* (London: Banner of Truth Trust, 1970), p. 371.

noteworthy that although they can answer the most difficult questions on philosophy, science and history, etc., they are often reduced to blundering fools by a simple question about the Bible!

Lifestyle is the expression of 'the thoughts and intentions of the heart'. The Bible distinguishes between the thoughts of the righteous and the wicked (*Prov.* 12:5; *Gen.* 6:5). Christ said, 'For out of the heart come evil thoughts, murder, adultery, sexual immorality, theft, false witness, slander' (*Matt.* 15:19). It is impossible to exaggerate the importance of guarding one's thoughts. Lady Montgomery, mother of the famous Field Marshall, was fond of quoting the saying, 'Guard well your thoughts, for thoughts are heard in heaven.' She wrote a tract with that title. 'You discern my thoughts from afar' (*Psa.* 139:2 cf. *Heb.* 4:12). On the subject of sexual temptations J. C. Ryle said,

> Flee the occasions of it, the company of those who might draw you into it, the places where you might be tempted to it. Read what our Lord says about it in Matthew 5:28. Be like holy Job: 'Make a covenant with your eyes' (*Job* 21:1). Flee *talking* of it . . . You cannot handle pitch and not be defiled. Flee the *thoughts* of it . . . Imagination is the hot-bed where this sin is often hatched. Guard your thoughts, and there is little fear about your deeds.[9]

Warning youth against the dangers of idleness, which may prove an occasion for sin, Ryle comments: 'If David

[9] Ibid., p. 385 f.

had not given occasion to the devil, by idling on his house-top at Jerusalem, he would probably never have seen Bathsheba, nor murdered Uriah.'[10]

Young people need more than warning and encouragement. They need the Saviour to guide and keep them. The Psalmist could say: 'For you, O Lord, are my hope, my trust, O LORD, from my youth . . . O God, from my youth you have taught me' (*Psa.* 71:5, 17).

As the childless Hannah prayed earnestly for a son, she vowed that if God gave her what her heart desired, she would give the child 'to the LORD all the days of his life' (*1 Sam.* 1:11). We may rest assured that the child Samuel was well taught from earliest days. Clearly he knew the Lord while still quite young for we read that 'the young man Samuel grew in the presence of the LORD', and that he 'continued to grow both in stature and in favour with the LORD' (*1 Sam.* 2:21, 26). As a child, Timothy was well acquainted with the Scriptures that were able to make him wise for salvation, having been taught by a godly mother and grandmother (*2 Tim.* 1:5; 3:15). It is good and God-honouring to dedicate one's life to the Saviour when young, rather than come to him when our years have been wasted and the flower of youth is withered and gone. It is a blessed thing to remember our Creator in the days of our youth, before the evil days come and the years draw near of which we will say, 'I have no pleasure in them' (cf. *Eccles.* 12:1). Christ is the Friend of youth. He welcomes children (*Matt.* 19:14). He could say to the Father, 'You made me trust you at my mother's breast . . .

---

[10] Ibid., p. 411

from my mother's womb you have been my God' (*Psa.* 22:9–10). At an early age he developed a keen interest in and an impressive knowledge of the truth (*Luke* 2:46–47). No one can guide and keep young people like Christ, who teaches them by his Word and Spirit, to love and serve him. Such young people know real joy, true fulfilment, and a noble and glorious aim in life – to glorify God in all they do.

The Lord uses human instrumentality in guiding the young. Many remember with thanksgiving the godly example of Christian parents or the ministry of teachers in church and school. In a day when many mothers are forced by circumstances to seek employment outside the home, it is important to retain the sense of 'togetherness' that ought to characterize family life: together in love, together in prayer. The godly pulpit and the godly home exercise a powerful influence. The devil hates them, so hold them fast.

> My son, keep your father's commandment, and forsake not your mother's teaching, bind them on your heart always, tie them round your neck. When you walk, they will lead you, when you lie down they will watch over you, and when you awake, they will talk with you (*Prov.* 6:20–22).

THE HAND THAT KEEPS US IN OLD AGE

Old age can mean the golden years or a time of infirmity. With greater leisure, there is more time for Bible study, reading, outdoor activities, hobbies, and for many precious hours with children and grandchildren. Husband and wife have more time to spend together: golden years indeed! Then there is the downside: failing health, pain, disease, a meagre pension, loneliness. For many, the approach of old age brings fear:

> The fear of being left alone, the fear of being a burden to loved ones, the fear of becoming a helpless invalid, the fear of losing one's grip, the fear of being imposed upon.[11]

There is also the fear of growing senile. We have all known Christians in this condition, unable to reason and even recall ordinary every day events, but yet able to remember passages of Scripture memorized sixty or seventy years earlier. This was a comfort to them and their loved ones, and a witness to others. Conscious of his own mortality, Paul writes, 'Wherefore we faint not; but though our outward man is decaying, yet our inward man is renewed day by day' (2 *Cor.* 4:16, ASV).

> When the will has forgotten the lifelong aim,
> And the mind can only disgrace its fame,
> And a man's uncertain of his own name—
> The power of the Lord shall fill this frame.
> R. D. Blackmore, *Dominus Illuminatio Mea*

The fears, triggered by advancing old age are not new. The Psalmist prayed, 'Do not cast me off in the time of old age; forsake me not when my strength is spent' (*Psa.* 71:9). He had experienced God's grace in his youth (*Psa.* 71:5–6) and wished that such blessing would extend to his old age. His strength may fail, but God will not fail him. In the Psalms the righteous are said to 'flourish like the palm tree and grow like a cedar in Lebanon . . . They still bear fruit in old age, they are ever full of sap and green' (*Psa.* 92:12–14). The godly in their old age display a certain resilience, a spiritual strength and buoyancy: the body may be weak, but faith is strong, and love and peace abound. They experience the nearness of God in their daily living.

There is nothing more desolate than a godless old age. They 'will not stand (*i.e.*, stand their ground) in the judgment' (*Psa.* 1:5). There are old people steeped in sin and defiant of God, and there are old people who are depending on their decency and honesty to ensure eternal bliss. The first class despise the cross, the second virtually ignore it and see it as unnecessary. On the judgment day, neither will stand.

Old age can be a time of extended service for Christ. There are a number of ways in which those who are retired can assist in the Lord's work, using their gifts and talents to the glory of God. In many of today's churches attention is focused on youth, but at times the elderly feel marginalized: this cannot be right.

The Bible teaches us to honour the aged; they have the experience of the years God has given them and their advice ought to be welcomed and heeded. They should know and feel they are a valued part of the church. Should they be confined to their homes the church must not forget about them and leave them in isolation for long periods of time. That is wrong.

Old age provides additional time for prayer and reflection. Referring to 'the golden years', Graham Miller writes:

> Eventide is the flowering time for the believer's life of prayer. He is free to devote more time to prayer. He wakens early and his waking thoughts are all turned into prayers. And this is a true vocation from the Lord.[12]

Through the prophet Isaiah, God addressed Israel with tender words:

> Listen to me, O house of Jacob, all the remnant of the house of Israel, who have been borne by me from before your birth, carried from the womb; even to your old age I am he, and to grey hairs I will carry you (*Isa.* 46:3–4).

A parent will carry a child while young, but soon the child must learn to walk unaided. For Israel, however, God's fatherly protection would be permanent, to the end of life.

E. J. Young notes here that the word translated 'old age' implies 'hoary old age' and that the verb 'carry' 'is used of the bearing of a heavy burden'.[12] God sustains his church in every age to the end of time: he carries his people collectively and individually. That is the word of the sovereign God: there lies our comfort and security for ever.

---

[11] Graham Miller, *The Treasury of His Promises* (Edinburgh: Banner of Truth Trust, 1986), p. 221.

[12] E. J. Young, *The Book of Isaiah* (Grand Rapids: Wm. B. Eerdmans, 1974), vol. 3, p. 222.

THE HAND THAT KEEPS US IN DEATH

Hearing an atheist weep uncontrollably over the dead body of the mother he loved so dearly, leaves an indelible impression on one's memory. Hopeless grief! When Loraine Boettner, that faithful and gracious exponent of the Reformed Faith, lay dying in 1989, he refused any artificial means to prolong his life, saying, 'I am ready to go.' In great pain and utter weakness he could only whisper his words. Carroll Fischer called to see him and Boettner whispered to him, 'There's a time to be born and a time to die. My time has come so don't feel bad. Just tell everyone how I loved the Lord and what I thought, and do not be sorrowful for me, but be sorrowful for those that don't know Jesus Christ.' In recording this testimony, Tony Mattia says, 'How one dies tells much about the reality of one's life.'[14] When William Cunningham, one of Scotland's greatest theologians, came to die, he was heard to say, 'I am going home quietly.'

Not all Christians, however, experience such comfort in death. Some are assailed by doubts and fears. That fine Christian poet, Christina Rossetti, was troubled by dark thoughts as her earthly life ebbed away. Her brother, William, who was with her, wondered how one who had loved to study the Bible and had longed so fervently for heaven, should in her last days be so troubled and dismayed. Such experience though unusual is not unique.

Some believers die peacefully; others experience desolation and distress. Why is this? A last attack by Satan? We cannot be sure. One thing is certain: at such times God's

[14] *The Banner of Truth*, April 1990.

fearful children are eternally secure in his sovereign hand (*John* 10:29; *Rom.* 8:38–39).

It is clear from Scripture that death is the penalty for sin, and that the human race became subject to death as a result of Adam's sin. Physical death symbolized the death of the soul. By nature we are 'dead in trespasses and sins' (*Eph.* 2:1). 'In Adam all die' (*1 Cor.* 15:22). Adam was the federal head of the human race and his guilt is imputed to his descendants. Not only so, but 'all mankind, descending from him by ordinary generation, sinned in him, and fell with him, in his first transgression' (*Westminster Shorter Catechism*, Q. and A. 16, cf. *Rom.* 5:12). At the time of the Fall, God said to Adam, 'You are dust, and to dust you shall return' (*Gen.* 3:19). Those words are not a mere declaration that death will naturally occur, as is sometimes understood at funerals.

That divine statement occurs in a curse and should not be taken out of its context. Such doctrine is wholly unacceptable to liberal theologians, and to evolutionary philosophers who see death as the end of man's existence. In their view, all that remains after death is the immortality of influence, which fades with each passing generation. Scripture flatly contradicts such a view of death when it states: 'It is appointed for man to die once, and after that comes judgment' (*Heb.* 9:27).

While our Lord tarries, all must die. Death ought not to be seen as a friend, but as an enemy, albeit a defeated enemy because of Christ's atoning death for the sins of his people: 'In Christ shall all be made alive' (*i.e.*, all whom he represents and who are joined to him by faith, *1 Cor.*

15:22). 'The last enemy to be destroyed is death' (1 Cor. 15:26). Here in this verse death is used in the fullest sense of the word: physical and spiritual. The reign of death (Rom. 5:14) will end at Christ's return. Then he will have put 'all his enemies under his feet' (1 Cor. 15:25). Because of this truth, death has been robbed of its sting for the believer. A broken law can no longer condemn, and the eventual abolition of death is assured. So with Paul the believer can echo the triumphant words of Hosea 13:14: 'Death is swallowed up in victory. O death, where is your victory? O death where is your sting ?' (1 Cor. 15:54–55).

Christians experience sorrow at times of bereavement: not to grieve would be a denial of our humanity. Their tears are in order. But the sorrow of Christians in times of bereavement is qualitatively different from that of un-believers. We 'sorrow not, even as the rest, who have no hope' (1 Thess. 4:13, ASV). We know that when we are 'away from the body' we are 'at home with the Lord' (2 Cor. 5:8). We know that our bodies will be raised at the Last Day to be like Christ's 'glorious body' (Phil. 3:21). We know that we will be reunited in heaven with loved ones who died in the Lord (2 Sam. 11:23; John 14:2-3). Above all, we know that we shall be in the immediate presence of our dear Saviour for ever (Rev. 22:4).

Such hope is a 'steadfast anchor of the soul' (Heb. 6:19). Dying may not be a pleasant experience, but the Christian need not fear death. Why are some Christians so loath to speak about death or to prepare themselves for it? It has been called a morbid subject. Going to be with the Lord, morbid?

William Grimshaw, a clergyman of the Church of England, preached the gospel courageously in eighteenth-century Yorkshire, often in the face of angry, stone-throwing crowds and in danger of his life. His 'holy and useful career', as J. C. Ryle described it, 'came to an end on the 7th April 1763'. As his life ebbed away, he said to a friend: 'My last enemy is come! The signs of death are upon me. But I am not afraid. No! No! Blessed be God, my hope is sure, and I am in his hands.' Later he said: 'I am quite exhausted; but I shall soon be home – for ever with the Lord – a poor miserable sinner redeemed by his blood.'[15] 'I am in his hands': that is true of all who die in the Lord.

[15] J. C. Ryle, *Christian Leaders of the Eighteenth Century* (Edinburgh: Banner of Truth, 1997), pp. 130–1.

6

THE HAND THAT GUIDES

Guidance can be a baffling subject for many. The need for guidance is recognized. But how is it obtained? The unconverted seek guidance in a variety of ways. Some turn to astrology, seeking guidance from the stars. It is dangerous to read horoscopes 'for fun'. Experience shows that sooner or later a person will be influenced by them. Kindred practices like palm reading also fall within the sphere of the occult, which reaches the ultimate in spiritism. In a godless, materialistic age, man, unable to suppress his innate religious instinct, turns increasingly to the occult for guidance and comfort. These are dark paths, designed by Satan and sign-posted to hell. God's Word warns against them. 'And when they say to you, "Enquire of the mediums and the necromancers who chirp and mutter", should not a people enquire of their God?' (*Isa.* 8:19). 'And beware lest you raise your eyes to heaven, and when you see the sun and the moon and the stars . . . you be drawn away and bow down to them and serve them' (*Deut.* 4:19). Any reverence for or trust in the stars is idolatry.

Christians, who shun such sinister ways, are often confused when it comes to following a safe and reliable path.

Various methods have been tried to obtain guidance. Someone with an important decision to make opens a Bible at random to see what verse first catches his eye. The Bible, however, is not some kind of spiritual lottery to be treated in such a random fashion. Granted, in one's daily reading of the Word, a certain passage or verse may appear supremely relevant to one's present need. We thank God that his Word continues to teach, reprove, correct, and train us in righteousness. Others who are determined to follow a certain course affirm confidently, 'The Lord told me . . .'; but God does not speak verbally to us independently of his Word, nor does he sign on the dotted line of our proposed plans and schemes. The Almighty cannot be manipulated by his creatures.

Little of value has been written on the subject of guidance and yet the Bible has much to say about this important subject.

GUIDANCE PROMISED

God has promised to guide his people. 'I will instruct you and teach you in the way you should go; I will counsel you with my eye upon you' (*Psa.* 32:8). Through the prophet Isaiah, God said to his people of old: 'The Lord will guide you continually and satisfy your desire in scorched places and make your bones strong, and you shall be like a watered garden, like a spring of water' (*Isa.* 58:11). The Psalmist prayed, 'Lead me and guide me' (*Psa.* 31:3); 'Lead me, O Lord, in your righteousness' (*Psa.* 5:8; cf. 27:11; 43:3). Repeatedly the Psalmist looks to God for guidance and gives voice to his confidence that

God will lead him. Regardless of his whereabouts this was true. 'If I take the wings of the morning and dwell in the uttermost parts of the sea, even there your hand shall lead me, and your right hand shall hold me' (*Psa.* 139:9).

We have seen that God is in complete control of his creation. Therefore it is wrong to speak of chance or luck. According to humanistic, evolutionary philosophy, we exist in a context solely of chance, in an environment devoid of ultimate meaning. We are seen as living in a meaningless, purposeless universe: nothing is fixed and final. From the standpoint of evolutionary philosophy, 'Man himself becomes an enigma, simply a chance emergent in a cosmos born of explosion and moving like all other animals toward death as his final end.'[1] That is a bleak, sombre view of reality. Ultimately it engenders pessimism.

How utterly different is the truth about God's relationship to his creation and the glorious destination to which all history moves. How good to know that this great God is mindful of the needs of his creatures, and that he loves his people with an everlasting love. Terms like 'chance' and 'luck' are really an expression of unbelief in God and should have no place in the vocabulary of the Christian. Such terms are utterly incompatible with the concept of divine guidance.

God's guidance extends to our actions and to our beliefs. 'The steps of a man are established (made firm) by the Lord, when he delights in his way' (*Psa.* 37:23). God has ordered the course of his life: there is nothing haphaz-

[1] Carl F. H. Henry, *op.cit.*, vol. 2, p. 334.

ard about it. Neither is he left to go forward in his own strength: 'For the LORD upholds him with his hand' (*Psa.* 37:24, NKJV). Commenting upon these words, J. A. Alexander writes: 'The participle, as usual, denotes continued action. God not only sustains him in particular emergencies, but is his habitual upholder.'[2]

We may know the divine guidance of God's Word. We have the promise that 'the Spirit of truth' will guide us 'into all the truth' (*John* 16:13). Christ prayed for his disciples: 'Sanctify them in the truth', adding, 'your word is truth' (*John* 17:17). Those who would by-pass the apostles and concentrate on 'the original Jesus' are sadly mistaken. The Holy Spirit led the apostles deeper and deeper into the knowledge of the truth, opening before them an ever-widening vista of truth. Besides, Christ also said of the Holy Spirit, 'He will glorify me, for he will take what is mine and declare it to you' (*John* 16:14). It is important to pray for the Spirit's guidance as we study the Scriptures; man's unaided reason is inadequate for the task. We need to pray, 'Open my eyes, that I may behold wondrous things out of your law' (*Psa.* 119:18).

We tend to forget our need of divine guidance. So often we make our plans without taking the sovereignty of God into consideration. His Word rebukes us. 'Come now, you who say, "Today or tomorrow we will go into such and such a town and spend a year there and trade and make a profit" – yet you do not know what tomorrow will bring . . . Instead you ought to say, "If the Lord wills, we will

---

[2] *The Psalms Translated and Explained* (Grand Rapids: Zondervan Publishing House, n.d.), p. 165.

live and do this or that"' (*James* 4:13-15). *Deo volente!* How seldom the letters 'DV' appear in church notices today.

GUIDANCE EXPERIENCED

In the Bible we have a number of examples of the personal experience of God's guidance. Abraham's steward knew the Lord's guidance when sent by his master to find a suitable wife for Isaac. Sharing the faith of Abraham, the servant prayed: 'O LORD, God of my master Abraham, please grant me success today and show steadfast love to my master Abraham' (*Gen.* 24:12). This unselfish prayer was accompanied by a request for a sign, which would indicate the young woman he should approach with the request that she become Isaac's wife. His prayer was answered, the sign was given and the servant, Laban, Bethuel, and Rebekah herself, recognized 'the hand of God' in the providence.

At an important stage in his life, David experienced divine guidance. Saul was dead and the time had come for David to reign. The kingdom was in a state of confusion. David was among the Philistines in the town of Ziklag (*1 Sam.* 27:6–7). The Philistines had defeated Israel and David now found himself in great difficulty. What was he to do? He 'enquired of the LORD, "Shall I go up into any of the cities of Judah?" And the LORD said to him, "Go up." David said, "To which shall I go up?" And he said, "To Hebron."' God gave him specific guidance and made it possible for him to go to Hebron, where he was anointed king over the house of Judah (*2 Sam.* 2:1–4). In this David is an example to us all. Those were David's best days when he lived close to God.

When King Hezekiah succeeded the idolatrous Ahaz, he set out to honour God and to follow him. Alfred Edersheim states that 'His policy was not to have any policy, but to trust in the living God, to obey his Word, and to follow his guidance.'[3] While Hezekiah placed his trust in God and looked solely to him for help and guidance, his reign was signally blessed.

There are times when God's guidance is so strong that it over-rules our wishes. Two examples from the New Testament come to mind. Philip had a remarkably fruitful ministry as he preached the gospel in Samaria (*Acts* 8:48). It took much courage and faith to approach the Samaritans, given the mutual detestation that existed between them and the Jews. Suddenly Philip was told to leave this scene of great joy and blessing and go instead to Gaza, a sixty-mile journey across desert land. Why such an abrupt change of scene and ministry? Like Abraham of old, he had received a command from God to go where God directed (*Acts* 8:26): like Abraham, he obeyed without asking questions. As he travelled that lonely desert road he saw the Ethiopian court official seated in his chariot. Then 'the Spirit said to Philip, "Go over and join this chariot"' (*Acts* 8:29). Obedience to God's word on Philip's part resulted in the conversion of the Ethiopian. God guided his servant every step of the way. When he received the command from the angel of the Lord and set

[3] Alfred Edersheim, *Bible History: Old Testament* (Peabody: Hendrickson Publishers, 1995), p. 911.

out for Gaza, he may well have wondered why he should leave the great awakening in Samaria and take this lonely desert road. In retrospect he would see the hand of God in his experience and praise his Name.

> Philip's unexpected departure from Samaria was ordained of God so that the gospel would come to a solitary Ethiopian. But what would the consequences be of Philip's testimony to the Ethiopian eunuch? What would the conversion of this man mean for Africa? Think of it: before a single European had been converted to Christ, this African, an important official in charge of all the treasury of Candace, queen of the Ethiopians, was to hear about the Saviour and trust in Christ, and take the glorious gospel home to that great continent.[4]

When Paul and Silas planned to go to Bithynia in northwest Asia Minor, 'the Spirit of Jesus did not allow them.' Later, 'a vision appeared to Paul in the night: a man of Macedonia [northern Greece] was standing there, urging him and saying, "Come over to Macedonia and help us."' Paul concluded that God had called them to preach the gospel there (*Acts* 16:7–10). In the Macedonian city of Philippi, Lydia was converted, and there, too, the apostles faced intense hostility, leading to imprisonment and the dramatic conversion of their jailer. As the end of our earthly life draws near, we can look back on those times when our plans were overturned, and God led us in another, and a better way.

---

[4] Geoffrey Thomas, *Philip and the Revival in Samaria* (Edinburgh: Banner of Truth, 2005), p. 96.

Samuel Rutherford's life witnessed many twists and turns, yet he never doubted the gracious Providence that attended his way. Mrs A. R. Cousin, who put some of his sweetest sayings into verse, has captured Rutherford's awareness of God's hand in his life.

> With mercy and with Judgment
> My web of time He wove,
> And aye the dews of sorrow
> Were lustred with His love,
> I'll bless the hand that guided,
> I'll bless the heart that plann'd,
> When throned where glory dwelleth
> In Immanuel's land.

Blessed is the one who can subscribe to those lines!

The prophet Jeremiah exclaims: 'I know, O LORD, that the way of man is not in himself, that it is not in man who walks to direct his steps' (*Jer.* 10:23), and Proverbs 20:24 echoes this truth: 'A man's steps are from the LORD; how then can man understand his way?' Did Joseph understand his way when searching for his brethren? (*Gen.* 37:14). Did Philip understand his way when he was moved from a wide sphere of Christian witness in Samaria, to take that desert road to Gaza? We do not know what a day may bring (*Prov.* 27:1), but the people of God need to remember that God's guiding hand is ever upon them.

In Old Testament times, God often spoke directly to men, by angels, visions and dreams. So it was in apostolic times too. That is no longer the case. We do not receive messages directly from heaven, nor do we possess the Urim and Thummin consulted by Israel's high priest in order to discover the will of God. All such communications are no longer necessary because we have the complete Word of God in the Scriptures. As we prayerfully study that Word and obey it we will know divine guidance.

Clearly we are not to sit back thinking that God will direct our steps without our trust in him and our loving obedience. God 'leads the humble in what is right, and teaches the humble his way' (*Psa.* 25:9). 'The steps of a man are established by the LORD, when he delights in his way' (*Psa.* 37:23). It is as we walk with the Lord that we feel his hand upon us. Abraham could say to his steward: 'The LORD, before whom I have walked' (*Gen.* 24:40). 'Enoch walked with God' (*Gen.* 5:22), and so did Noah (*Gen.* 6:9). We too have received an exhortation to walk with God: 'Therefore, as you received Christ Jesus the Lord, so walk in him . . . ' (*Col.* 2:6).

God's Providence does not relieve us of our responsibility.

> For he who has set limits to our life has at the same time entrusted to us its care; he has provided means and helps to preserve it; he has also made us able to foresee dangers; that they may not overwhelm us unaware, he has offered precautions and remedies. Now it is very clear what our duty is: thus, if the Lord has committed to us the protection of our life, our duty is to protect it; if he offers helps, to use them; if he forewarns us of dangers,

not to plunge headlong; if he makes remedies available, not to neglect them. . . God's providence does not always meet us in its naked form, but God in a sense clothes it with the means employed.[5]

When faced with an important decision some practical questions will help. Is this right? Clearly, employment by a gambling consortium would be wrong, and for a Christian to marry an unbeliever would be wrong. Have I the ability to undertake this work? Have I the desire to do it? And finally, is the door of Providence open to me? In facing important decisions, the Christian should pray earnestly that God will guide him in his thinking, and then think carefully before making the decision. God does not abandon his child at such a time.

GUIDANCE NEGLECTED

Abraham knew God's guidance when he left Haran to go to a land that God would show him. Later, at a time of famine, he went down to Egypt, pretending that Sarah his wife was his sister (she was, in fact, his half-sister) thereby putting her at great risk as well as practising deceit. It would seem that this was a precipitate decision, taken without seeking divine guidance. Similarly, facing famine in Israel, Elimelech took his wife and his two sons and went to live for a time in Moab. There he died and his sons married heathen women. There was a prohibition against admitting Moabites into the congregation of

[5] John Calvin, *Institutes of the Christian Religion* (London: S.C.M. Press, Battles' translation, n.d.), I.17.4.

Israel and the descendants of marriage with a Moabite were not to be admitted to the tenth generation (*Deut.* 23:3): this was because of Moab's hostility to the Israelites at the time of the Exodus from Egypt. Later, Elimelech's two sons, Mahlon and Chilion, died. It is hard to believe that Elimelech, whose name means 'My God is King', sought divine guidance before taking his family to heathen territory. Those who remained at home, found that the famine was not so extreme as to make life there impossible. Elimelech was not in great need when he departed, for he 'went out full' (*Ruth* 1:21). Matthew Henry observes that if others had followed Elimilech's example, Canaan would have been depopulated, adding:

> It is an evidence of a discontented, distrustful, unstable spirit, to be weary of the place in which God has set us, and to be for leaving it immediately whenever we meet with any inconvenience in it. It is folly to think of escaping that cross which, being laid in our way, we ought to take up. It is our wisdom to make the best of that which is, for it is seldom that changing our place is mending it.[6]

However we view Elimelech's action, it is hard to justify it and Moab was not a place where a godly Hebrew should have taken his family. That God in his mercy overruled the situation for good, in no way excuses Elimilech's action. It is always costly to neglect God's guidance and act in an independent spirit of self-interest.

King Saul 'broke faith with the LORD in that he did not keep the command of the LORD, and also consulted a

---

[6] Matthew Henry's *Commentary.*

medium, seeking guidance. He did not seek guidance from the LORD. Therefore the LORD put him to death and turned the kingdom over to David . . . ' (1 *Chron.* 10:13–14). He died for his 'breach of faith' and also because 'he did not seek guidance from the LORD.'

King Asa who was responsible for a measure of religious reform in Judah, erred gravely when he entered into an alliance with the king of Syria and was rebuked by Hanani the Seer for not relying on the Lord his God. 'In the thirty-ninth year of his reign Asa was diseased in his feet, and his disease became severe. Yet even in his disease he did not seek the LORD, but sought help from physicians' (2 *Chron.* 16:7, 12). Seeking medical help in a time of illness does not preclude prayer to our heavenly Father. In every aspect of life we ought to rely on God.

Through Isaiah the prophet God rebuked his people for seeking protection from Egypt and thereby adding sin to sin. '"Ah, stubborn children", declares the LORD, "who carry out a plan, but not mine, and who make an alliance, but not of my Spirit, that they may add sin to sin; who set out to go down to Egypt, without asking for my direction. . . "' (*Isa.* 30:1–2). 'Adding sin to sin': first by acting without divine guidance, and then by making an alliance or seeking a covering (literally 'blanket') not of God's Spirit (*i.e.*, seeking protection from Pharaoh, not from the LORD). Planning without God! 'Stubborn children'!

The prophet Jeremiah bewailed the fact that those who were to shepherd the people of God failed dismally in their task. 'For the shepherds are stupid and do not enquire of the LORD; therefore they have not prospered, and all their flock is scattered' (*Jer.* 10:21). Zephaniah foretold the judgement of 'those who have turned back from following the LORD, and who do not seek the LORD or enquire of him' (*Zeph.* 1:6). These were people who were content to go through life without considering God and his will for them.

It is abundantly plain from God's Word that to neglect his guidance is sinful. When Christians take decisions, motivated by self-interest and with no thought of God, they sin. It is all too easy to slip into this sin. Let us repent of this godless practice.

GUIDANCE SPURNED

In any understanding of reality one's initial presupposition is crucial. There are only two such presuppositions: either God is or God is not. The Bible does not try to prove the existence of God. It simply says that God *is*. What are the first words that you read when you open a Bible? 'In the beginning God . . .' At that moment you are either a believer (at least intellectually) or an unbeliever. Your initial presupposition will determine your view of the universe, man, history, guidance, right and wrong. Your outlook on such matters will either be God-centred or man-centred; if the latter, it is meaningless to think of guidance in the sense that Scripture speaks about it: no God, no guiding hand.

Humanistic, evolutionary philosophers, who have shaped the thinking of millions, insist on the absolute autonomy of man. The revealed religion of the Bible is rejected as a myth of mammoth proportions. On this

view, there is no ultimate truth, no eternal purpose behind
the universe. Man is seen as self-sufficient. Reliance on
external authority is said to destroy man's creative
instinct. Man can cope without gods while freely fashion-
ing his life and interpreting reality for himself. The irony
of this position is that in rejecting God as the source and
giver of reason, man turns to irrationality as he speaks of
chance. If we live in an environment lacking ultimate
meaning and goodness, there is no anchor for the soul
and the gloom of nihilism awaits us. Thank God such a
philosophy is not true. Yet those who think along such
lines spurn God's existence, God's authority, and God's
guidance. They say in their hearts: 'There is no God' (*Psa.*
14:1).

One does not have to be of the number of godless
philosophers to be guilty of the sin of spurning God's
truth. Man's sinful heart is intrinsically rebellious. God's
promise to teach us the way that we should go, is followed by the command, 'Be not like a horse or a mule,
without understanding, which must be curbed with bit
and bridle. . . ' (*Psa.* 32:8–9). The mule was a 'type' of
stubborn persistence in sinning; and in Jeremiah 8:6 we
read: 'Everyone turns to his own course, like a horse
plunging headlong into battle.' On that verse the
Lutheran commentator, Theodore Laetsch, says:

> Eagerly, impatiently they all hurry to their idols, as the
> horse rushes headlong into battle. We need but watch the
> crowds struggling to get into the temples of amusement,
> there to offer their money and their time to the idols of

this world (*1 John* 2:16–17), and we shall see one of the modern forms of ancient idolatry and deception.[7]

That is practical atheism, living as if God did not exist, and so typical of our own generation. In Isaiah 63 we read how God led his people in the time of Moses: 'the Spirit of the LORD gave them rest. So you led your people, to make for yourself a glorious name' (*Isa.* 63:14). Earlier in that chapter we read, 'But they rebelled and grieved his Holy Spirit' (63:10). God's gracious guidance was repeatedly spurned.

Ahaz ascended the throne of Judah at the age of twenty-five. When the forces of Syria and of Israel went to make war against Jerusalem, 'the heart of Ahaz and the heart of his people shook as the trees of the forest shake before the wind' (*Isa.* 7:1–2). Isaiah was sent by God to assure Ahaz that there was nothing to fear (*Isa.* 7:4). His enemies' plans would fail. Ahaz must trust in God and not in some earthly alliance. E. J. Young comments here: 'When God says "Fear not", there is nothing to fear.'[8] But Ahaz was not listening. God now speaks to Ahaz directly, offering a sign to reassure him of God's faithfulness. God's prophet urged him: 'Ask a sign of the LORD your God . . . ' (*Isa.* 7:10). But Ahaz remained stubborn and defiant: 'I will not ask, and I will not put the LORD to the test' (*Isa.* 7:12). His refusal was clothed with the pious language of a hypocrite. He thought he knew better than God! And so, by his wilful rejection of divine guidance, he ensured the

[7] Theodore Laetsch, *Jeremiah* (Saint Louis: Concordia Publishing House, 1965), p. 107.

[8] E. J. Young, *Isaiah*, vol. 1, p. 272.

very destruction he wished to escape. Franz Delitzsch observes: 'In that very hour, in which Isaiah was standing before Ahaz, the fate of Jerusalem was decided for more than two thousand years.'[9] Spurning divine guidance is an act of unbelief and shows a complete and utter lack of trust in God.

There are times when young men and women spurn divine guidance without realizing it. That in no way lessens the sin. When the counsel and advice of a godly father or mother is rejected, divine guidance is spurned. Parents have God-given authority to teach and train their children. The Bible warns young people against ignoring their counsel. 'Listen to your father who gave you life, and do not despise your mother when she is old' (*Prov.* 23:22). 'Hear, O sons, a father's instruction, and be attentive, that you may gain insight' (*Prov.* 4:1; cf. *Prov.* 10:1, 15). Some who ignored the wise counsel of a parent, have paid dearly for their sin throughout the rest of their lives: they spurned divine guidance. God can use the counsel of a parent, a pastor, or a friend to show us the way we should go.

There is a striking example of God using human agency to provide guidance in the experience of Calvin the Reformer. When William Farel learned that the young author of the *Institutes of the Christian Religion* (the first edition was published in 1536 when Calvin was just 26) was staying overnight in Geneva, *en route* to Strasburg, he visited him and exhorted him to remain in Geneva as a teacher. Calvin insisted that his place was that of a

[9] Quoted by Edward J. Young, *Isaiah*, vol.1, p. 281.

scholar at his desk. Farel, in anger, threatened him with the curse of God if he turned his back on needy Geneva. Calvin describes this encounter thus:

> William Farel detained me at Geneva, not so much by counsel and exhortation, as by a dreadful imprecation, which I felt to be as if God had from heaven laid his mighty hand upon me to arrest me . . . And after having learned that my heart was set upon devoting myself to private studies, for which I wished to keep myself free from other pursuits, and finding that he gained nothing by entreaties, he proceeded to utter an imprecation that God would curse my retirement, and the tranquillity of the studies which I sought, if I should refuse to give assistance, when the necessity was so urgent. By this imprecation I was so stricken with terror, that I desisted from the journey which I had undertaken.[10]

That was a crucial turning point in the Reformation of the sixteenth century, which Calvin would realize in the course of time.

If we earnestly and prayerfully seek God's guidance, we shall have it, not perhaps in the form we expected or wanted, but according to our need. Perhaps this is what Alexander Vinet meant when he said: 'To have sought God's will is to have found it.'[11]

---

[10] John Calvin, 'Preface', *Commentary on the Psalms*.
[11] Quoted by Graham Miller, *op.cit.*, p. 211

7

THE HAND THAT CHASTENS

Terms like 'punishment' and 'chastisement' are not popular today. Sociologists tend to speak about rehabilitation (not that that should be excluded), while discarding the idea of punishment for wrongdoing. Liberal theologians, influenced by the prevailing influence of humanistic philosophy, think and speak in similar terms. They reject the doctrine of the penal substitutionary death of Christ: the idea that Jesus was punished for our sins is repugnant to them. They like to think of God purely in terms of love. But God is one, and none of his perfections (also termed attributes) should be considered in isolation. God is indeed our loving, heavenly Father, but Scripture shows that there is no conflict between the ideas of God as Father and as Judge.

Our Lord's teaching makes this abundantly clear. In the New Testament, we see Jesus as the Lamb and as the Lion (*John* 1:29; *Rev.* 5:5). The apostle Peter stressed the unity of God's nature as Father and Judge when he wrote: 'And if you call on him as Father who judges impartially according to each one's deeds, conduct yourselves with fear throughout the time of your exile' (1 *Pet.* 1:17). In the Bible we see God as King, and Father and Judge, all entirely compatible. Geerhardus Vos writes:

It is necessary to keep these two elements of the love of God and of His heavenly majesty jointly in mind, in order to avoid one-sidedness; they must likewise be conceived as interacting. God's majesty and greatness impart a specific character to the divine love. Love from and towards man are different from the same feeling as exercised between God and man.[1]

All too often God's love is reduced to the level of human love, which is a gift from God, but is not to be equated with God's love for us or our experience of that love. God's law is a law of love; his discipline is also of love. He disciplines his children for their good. Early in Scripture we see God disciplining his people when they displeased him. This was fatherly training. Our word 'discipline' comes from the Latin *disciplina,* implying a process of learning, and so we speak of a subject of academic study as a 'discipline'.

To Israel God said: 'Know then in your heart that, as a man disciplines his son, the LORD your God disciplines you' (*Deut.* 8:5). The Psalmist could say: 'Blessed is the man whom you discipline, O LORD, and whom you teach out of your law' (*Psa.* 94:12; cf. *Lev.* 26:28; *Hos.* 10:10). There is a striking statement in Amos 3:2: 'You only have I known of all the families of the earth; therefore I will punish you for all your iniquities.' God does not punish our sins in a legal sense: that he did fully at Calvary. The chastisements he brings upon his people are to be understood as the loving corrections of a merciful and tender-hearted father.

[1] Geerhardus Vos, *Biblical Theology* (Edinburgh: Banner of Truth, 1975), p. 369.

CHASTENING AND DISOBEDIENCE

Clearly God chastens his people when they disobey him. We think of the experiences of Israel when led by Moses out of Egypt and through the wilderness. Again and again they 'provoked the LORD to wrath'. They longed for 'the fish. . . the cucumbers, the melons, the leeks and onions and the garlic' of Egypt, conveniently forgetting the lash of the taskmaster's whip! (*Num.* 11:5). They dared to ask: 'Can God spread a table in the wilderness? He struck the rock so that water gushed out and streams overflowed. Can he also give bread to provide meat for his people?' (*Psa.* 78:19–20). 'Can God'! They questioned the power and ability of God, and 'his anger rose against Israel' (*Psa.* 78:21).

When Moses was absent, they prevailed on Aaron to supply them with gods to lead them. Weakly he obeyed and made a golden calf, saying: 'These are your gods, O Israel, who brought you up out of the land of Egypt' (*Exod.* 32:1–4). Only for Moses' earnest intercession, God's wrath would have consumed the people (*Exod.* 32:10–14). Moses himself incurred God's displeasure more than once and was chastened for his disobedience. When he failed to circumcise Zipporah's son, possibly because of her reluctance, we read that 'the LORD met him and sought to put him to death' (*Exod.* 4:24).

The neglect of the divinely appointed sign of the covenant of peace with God was a serious delinquency, especially to him who was to be the leader and lawgiver of the holy people. It was meet that the austere perfection of the divine holiness should be made known to Moses. It was necessary at this stage of his experience that he should learn that God is in earnest when he speaks, and will assuredly perform all that he has threatened. Hence the Lord sought to kill him [AV rendering], probably by some disease or sudden stroke, which threatened immediate death.[2]

God's chastening was his method of restoring a wayward people or individual. 'I have heard Ephraim grieving, "You have disciplined me, and I was disciplined, like an untrained calf; bring me back that I may be restored, for you are the LORD my God' (*Jer.* 31:18). How often the Christian needs to make that his prayer: 'Bring me back that I may be restored'! Left to himself he wanders away. Only the Lord can turn us away from sin to faith and obedience.

There are situations in a believer's life that call for divine chastisement. David had a fairly smooth course as king until after his sin with Bathsheba: then his troubles multiplied. Open sin will invite God's rod.

Let the believer bemire himself with lust, or put forth his hand unto violence, or speak lying or lascivious words – let him give great and scandalous cause to the enemy to blaspheme, – and, as surely as he is the Lord's child, his back shall smart for it.[3]

Another cause of chastisement is backsliding, those times in the believer's life when devotions are forgotten,

[2] J. G. Murphy, *Commentary on the Book of Exodus* (Minneapolis, Klock & Klock, 1979 reprint), p. 53.

[3] C. H. Spurgeon, in his precious book, *The Saint and His Saviour* (London: Hodder and Stoughton, 1884), p. 431.

sin is unconfessed, and the worship of God is neglected. When prayer and the Word of God are neglected, communion with the Saviour is lost and the Holy Spirit is grieved.

When the Christian is ashamed of Christ, hiding his colours and compromising on matters of principle, Christ is ashamed of him. The Christian has denied his Lord, as Peter once did. When idolatry is practiced, Christ withdraws. He will not tolerate rivals. Anything that comes before Christ is an idol. It may take the form of family, business, fashion, sport, pleasure, or earthly security: these must never have pre-eminence in our lives: their rightful place is beneath Christ's royal sceptre.

CHASTENING AND LOVE

It is common for cynics to represent the God who chastens as a harsh, unloving tyrant. Nothing could be further from the truth. Scripture consistently sees God's discipline in the context of love. So in Proverbs 3:11–12 God says: 'My son, do not despise the LORD's discipline or be weary of his reproof, for the LORD reproves him whom he loves, as a father the son in whom he delights.' The earthly father, looking to the heavenly Father and exercising his God-given responsibility to discipline and instruct his children (*Eph.* 6:4), will take to heart the word, 'whoever spares the rod hates his son, but he who loves him is diligent to discipline him' (*Prov.* 23:24; cf. 22:15; 23:13). He will be equally careful to avoid excessive discipline, for Ephesians 6:4 also gives the command: 'Fathers, do not provoke your children to anger.' Children must not be driven to exasperation by constant heavy-handed chastisement. We live in a day when there is little or no discipline in the home, and sadly this is sometimes the case in Christian homes. Undisciplined children will have no respect for authority in the home, the church, the school and in society. What a heavy price we are paying for indiscipline and the modern rejection of the concept of punishment for wrongdoing. This malaise begins in the home and only there can it be counteracted.

When Christians feel the rod of God's displeasure it is a sure sign of his love for them and a confirmation of their membership in his family (*Prov.* 3:11–12). Under the guidance of the Holy Spirit, the writer to the Hebrews adds:

> It is for discipline that you have to endure. God is treating you as sons. For what son is there whom his father does not discipline? If you are left without discipline, in which all have participated, [i.e. all sons], then you are illegitimate children and not sons. Besides this, we have had earthly fathers who disciplined us and we respected them. Shall we not much more be subject to the Father of spirits and live. For they disciplined us for a short time as it seemed best to them, but he disciplines us for our good, that we may share his holiness (*Heb.* 12:5–10).

Thank God for discipline! Without it we would not be his children. In discipline we have the sure token that we belong to God's family. We accepted the correction of earthly fathers and respected them. Sometimes they may have made mistakes in deciding on the kind of discipline we needed, but they did what 'seemed best to them'. Our heavenly Father, in perfect wisdom and love, will always impose the discipline that is for our good: all he does is perfect. William H. Green of Princeton wrote: 'The rod is in a loving Father's hand: its strokes are not capriciously nor unkindly given, they are administered solely for our good.'[4] Discipline, then, is the sure sign that we are God's children. In Scripture we learn that illegitimate children were excluded from 'the assembly of the LORD' (*Deut.* 23:2).[5] They had no standing in family or church.

In the light of God's Word, it is important to see discipline as the expression and proof of his love for us, and of our standing as his children and therefore 'heirs of God and fellow heirs with Christ' (*Rom.* 8:17). Chastisement demonstrates God's faithfulness to his warnings and to his promises. When we consider our sin, is it not a marvel that the chastisement is so light?

CHASTENING AND SELF-EXAMINATION

Discipline is never pleasant and often painful. However, for the Christian who is 'exercised' or 'trained' by it there comes a rich harvest, 'the peaceful fruit of righteousness' (*Heb.* 12:11). Truly 'emergencies are the making of some men, and the destruction of others . . . Under the pressure of sore affliction men are in danger of falling into one of two extremes. The first is that of repining and murmuring

---

[4] William H. Green, *The Argument of the Book of Job Unfolded* (Edinburgh: Banner of Truth, 1999), p. 81.

[5] There are differing interpretations of this verse, e.g., debarred from membership, debarred from holding office, etc. Whatever view one takes, it is clear that illicit 'unions' are abhorred by God and that he intends his people to be aware of this.

at the divine allotment: the other is that of bearing it in a spirit of stoical indifference.'[6] We have all witnessed that shrug of the shoulders accompanied by the comment, 'That's life!' To react in that way is to 'despise' the chastening of the Lord. There has been no self-examination, no spiritual stocktaking, no serious, prayerful response.

In every affliction suffered and in all adversity experienced discipline is present. In such times God is speaking to us and it behoves us to listen. Then the affliction becomes a blessing and we know by experience the promised righteousness and peace. We are reminded of words in Isaiah 32:17: 'And the effect of righteousness will be peace, and the result of righteousness quietness and trust for ever.' This tranquillity of spirit is radically different from the slumber that induces a false sense of security. It is produced by the Spirit of God and has no end.

In the First Epistle of Peter, the apostle reminds us of God's design in the trials we face: just as gold is tested and purified by fire, so our faith is purified through the endurance of trials (*1 Pet.* 1:6–7). In a similar vein James writes: 'Blessed is the man who remains steadfast under trial, for when he has stood the test he will receive the crown of life which God has promised to those who love him' (*James* 1:12). However dark the night, the Christian's prospects are always bright.

The truth that affliction is in itself a discipline is well illustrated in the experience of Job, an historical person (*Ezek.* 14:14; *James* 5:11) and possibly a contemporary of the patriarchs. At a time of family festivity, the calamitous

---

[6] William H. Green, *op.cit.*, pp. 73, 86.

storm burst upon him. Disaster followed disaster: in a matter of hours he lost all his property and, worst of all, his children. These tragedies were followed by his suffering a painful and chronic disease.

Job saw the sovereign 'hand of God' in his afflictions but was not aware of the hand of Satan, who tried to crush him in an attempt to make him curse God (*Job* 1:11). Satan, the arch-cynic, was allowed to do his worst against Job within *limits* (*Job* 1:12; 2:6). Later in redemption history, he was allowed to do his worst against God's Son *without* limits, but again he failed. Christ is therefore 'the pioneer and perfecter of our faith' (*Heb.* 12:2, RSV). 'It is on him . . . that in every age the gaze of faith is focused. He alone evokes and stimulates faith; and it is because he is the pioneer of our salvation (*Heb.* 2:10) that he is the author of our faith.'[7]

Job's thoughts centred on God, and ultimately he was right for it was the hand of God through Satan that was laid so heavily upon him. As Calvin says: 'Satan is clearly under God's power, and is so ruled by his bidding as to be compelled to render him service.'[8] It is chilling to read God's address to Satan: 'Behold, all that he has is in your hand', and, 'Behold, he is in your hand.'

Job faced this vicious and prolonged assault without the comforting promises and assurances that God's people now have in his Word. Truths familiar to us were unknown to him. As he sank deeper and deeper into an abyss of bitterness and sorrow, he never once reproached

---

[7] Philip E. Hughes, *Hebrews*, p. 522.
[8] John Calvin, *Institutes*, I:14:17.

his God. Through this sore discipline Job was to learn to trust and honour God as never before. As he repented of his complaints and murmurings, the last vestiges of self-righteousness were removed. Then there was uncritical acceptance of God's providential dealings with him, an acceptance that went beyond mere submission. Job had learned that the ways of God are inscrutable; it is not for us to ask 'Why?' God never answered Job's oft-repeated 'Why?' Job's piety had been deepened as in true repentance he cried: 'I had heard of you by the hearing of the ear, but now my eye sees you; therefore I despise myself in dust and ashes (*Job* 42:5–6). This depth of contrition became the summit of his piety. He saw God and himself in an altogether new light. God had come close to him. The discipline had accomplished its purpose. He had been 'trained' by it, had reflected on it and learned vital lessons. 'Behold', writes James, 'we consider those blessed who remained steadfast. You have heard of the steadfastness of Job, and you have seen the purpose of the Lord, how the Lord is compassionate and merciful' (*James* 5:11). 'The purpose of the Lord'! God always has a purpose when he chastens his children. His chastisements may be severe, but they are never meaningless: he always has a purpose of grace to accomplish.

This truth has been repeatedly illustrated in the history of the church. In 1552, five young men were arrested in Lyon on returning from their studies in Lausanne. They were imprisoned for their acceptance of Protestant doctrine. On the 10th of June that year, Calvin wrote to them assuring them that every effort was being made at the highest level to secure their release. But these efforts failed and the young men were executed by the Inquisition. Their martyrdom caused much sorrow in Reformed circles, and Calvin alluded to it several times in his correspondence. From prison these young men had written to the church of Geneva:

> Very dear brothers in Jesus Christ, since you have been informed of our captivity and the fury which drives our enemies to persecute and afflict us, we felt it would be good to let you know of the liberty of our spirit and of the wonderful assistance and consolation which our good Father and Saviour gives us in these dark prison cells. . . Further, we are bold to say and affirm that we shall derive more profit in this school of our salvation than has been the case in any place where we have studied, and we testify that this is the true school of the children of God in which they learn more than the disciples of the philosophers ever did in their universities. [9]

Their letter was read to the 'Congregation of the Brethren' on Friday, 15 July 1552. In it can be seen an acknowledgment of the gracious purpose of God in times of testing and trial.

Not only are individual believers chastened in accordance with God's sovereign purpose, but also churches can be disciplined for misconduct and unfaithfulness. This happened to the church at Corinth because the members were guilty of partaking of the Lord's Supper 'in an unworthy manner' (*1 Cor.* 11:27). In that case they ate and drank judgement on themselves (*1 Cor.* 11:29). And Paul adds: 'But when we are judged by the Lord, we are disciplined so that we may not be condemned with the world' (*1 Cor.* 11:32). Such judgement, as Herman Ridderbos reminds us, 'is meant as a chastisement and as a stimulus for subjecting itself [i.e., the church] to a searching examination.'[10] At Corinth many became 'weak and ill, and some died' (*1 Cor.* 11:30). The members of the church could see this judgement, and Paul tells them that God has a merciful purpose in this affliction, that they 'may not be condemned with the world.'

Such chastisement was a token of God's grace. Churches need to be reminded that there are times when they may richly deserve God's chastening rod. What does his Word say about squabbling? 'But if you bite and devour one another, watch out that you are not consumed by one another' (*Gal.* 5:15). What does it say about miserly giving? 'Whoever sows sparingly will also reap sparingly, and whoever sows bountifully will also reap bountifully. Each one must give as he has made up his mind, not reluctantly or under compulsion, for God loves a cheerful giver' (*2 Cor.* 9:6–7). We all need to keep this counsel in mind.

CHASTENING AND HOLINESS

We have seen that God always has a purpose when he chastens his children: that they should be holy. The writer

---

[9] *The Register of the Company of Pastors of Geneva in the time of Calvin*, edited by Philip E. Hughes (Grand Rapids: Wm. B. Eerdmans, 1966), pp. 191 f.

[10] Herman Ridderbos, *Paul*, pp. 552 f.

to the Hebrews having discussed discipline as a proof of sonship and stating that such discipline is 'for our good', adds, 'that we may share his holiness' (*Heb.* 12:10). When life runs smoothly, we can easily lose the desire for holiness. It is then that God's fatherly discipline weans us from seeking earthly security and enables us to look trustfully to him alone for comfort and blessing. The redeemed are 'those who are sanctified' (*Heb.* 2:11), set apart for holiness.

God not only uses the rod of adversity to promote holiness; he may also withdraw the sense of his presence from his children. The Psalmist declared: 'You hid your face, I was dismayed' (*Psa.* 30:7). God had withdrawn the sense of his presence and favour and the Psalmist was confounded and perplexed.

> Why dost Thou shade Thy lovely face? oh, why
> Doth that eclipsing hand so long deny
> The sunshine of Thy soul-enlivening eye?

> Without that light, what light remains in me?
> Thou art my life, my way, my light; in Thee
> I live, I move, and by Thy beams I see.

> Thou art my life; if Thou but turn away,
> My life's a thousand deaths: Thou art my way;
> Without Thee, Lord, I travel not, but stray.
> *Francis Quarles*

At times God does hide his face and for good reason. If we offend our Saviour by thought or action, we will lose the sweet sense of his presence.

There are, however, times when God hides his face in order to try our faith. When that happens, hope languishes, conscience accuses, and spirits sink. The Bible seems like a dead letter and prayer becomes mechanical. The soul is weak, confused, agitated. Spurgeon says: 'In proportion as the Master's presence is delightful, his absence is mournful.'[11] Then the believer begins to realize afresh how precious Christ is to his soul, how sweet is his presence and how desirable is his favour. With Job he can say, 'Oh, that I were as in the months of old, as in the days when God watched over me, when his lamp shone upon my head, and by this light I walked through darkness . . . ' (*Job* 29:2-3). The one who walks close to God feels his absence most keenly. What joy there is when the Saviour draws near again and precious fellowship with him is restored. The apparent absence caused by his withdrawal for a season has proved a blessing. It must not be thought that such times of testing are typical of Christian experience, but they can and do occur when our loving heavenly Father would draw us closer to himself and embrace us in tender mercy.

> Before I was afflicted I went astray, but now I keep your word . . . It is good for me that I was afflicted, that I might learn your statutes (*Psa.* 119:67, 71).

Christian reader, is Christ precious to you? Do you yearn for his presence? In Bunyan's *Pilgrim's Progress*, Mr Standfast says: 'I have loved to hear my Lord spoken of, and wherever I have seen the print of his shoe in the earth,

[11] C. H. Spurgeon, *The Saint and his Saviour*, p. 387.

there I have coveted to set my foot too.' And the Scottish Covenanter, Samuel Rutherford, wrote:

> Christ inquired not, when He began to love me, whether I was fair, or black or sun-burnt; love taketh what it may have. He loved me before this time, I know; but now I have the flower of his love; His love is come to a fair bloom, like a young rose opened. . . it casteth a strong and fragrant smell. I want nothing but ways of expressing Christ's love. . . O for a year's lease of the sense of His love without a cloud to try what Christ is! O for the coming of the Bridegroom! Oh, when shall I see the Bridegroom and the Bride meet in the clouds and kiss each other!. . . O time, time! how dost thou torment the souls that would be swallowed up of Christ's love, because thou movest so slowly![12]

Those words remind us of Song of Solomon 6:3: 'I am my beloved's and my beloved is mine.' Is there anything remotely like that in your experience? You believe in the deity of Christ, in his incarnation, substitutionary death, resurrection, his present reign, and his return as Judge. But do you *love* him? Does your heart go out to him? Is he precious to you? True holiness expresses itself in love for the Saviour. There is nothing supine or timorous about such love; on the contrary it strengthens one's loyalty to Christ. The truth will be staunchly yet graciously defended and error faithfully exposed.

Devotion to Christ will be increasingly manifest in the believer's life. When Scripture describes the status of the

---

[12] *Letters of Samuel Rutherford* (Edinburgh: Banner of Truth, 1984; reprinted 2006), Letter 130.

Christian, his standing before God, it also shows how this affects his life. There is what we term the *Indicative* and there is the *Imperative*. In Romans 6:11 believers are said to be 'dead to sin': that is the Indicative. Then we read, 'Let not sin therefore reign in your mortal bodies' (*Rom.* 6:12): that is the Imperative (cf. *Col.* 3:3–10). Having described how at Christ's return, the creation is to be renewed, the apostle Peter adds: 'Since all these things are thus to be dissolved, what sort of people ought you to be in lives of holiness and godliness' (2 *Pet.* 3:10–11). Doctrine is always related to conduct.[13]

The connection between doctrine and life cannot be stressed too strongly. Some Christians fail here. They will vigorously debate the finer points of doctrine, and defend orthodoxy, but they have little awareness of the practical implications of what they believe. This failure becomes evident in a deplorable elasticity of conscience, painfully witnessed in soured family relationships, dubious business dealings, and a cavalier attitude to legal requirements. They know the truth intellectually but do not 'walk in the truth' (3 *John* 4). Their Christian testimony in the home and community is tarnished and ineffective; God is dishonoured and the Holy Spirit is grieved. In Galatians 2:14 we read of those who 'walked not uprightly according to the truth of the gospel' (KJV), quite literally, their walk was not 'orthodox' (from Greek *orthos*, straight and *doxa*, opinion). There must be an orthodoxy of life as well as of doctrine.

[13] J. I. Packer says that ethics should never be studied independently of doctrine, nor doctrine independently of ethics. *Collected Shorter Writings* (Carlisle: Paternoster Press, 1998), Vol. 2, p. 364.

True holiness is characterized by loving obedience to God's commands and fervent love of the Saviour. That is what it means to 'share' in God's holiness, and without this holiness 'no one will see the Lord' (*Heb.* 12:10, 14). To that end God in grace and love disciplines his children, preparing them to dwell with him in glory. He employs his rod and his staff, the one to rule and the other to support, correcting by adversity and upholding by grace. Therein is our comfort.

8

THE HAND THAT BLESSES

God's blessings are his many gifts, both material and spiritual. His blessings come in various ways and in different forms. When he created the sea and land creatures, he 'blessed them, saying, "Be fruitful and multiply and fill the waters in the seas, and let birds multiply on the earth"' (*Gen.* 1:22). By that blessing he bestowed the powers necessary for the continuance and increase of life. That was a word of power that made possible what God commanded and that same enabling power continues to this day. When God created man, male and female, he 'blessed them. And God said to them, "Be fruitful and multiply and fill the earth and subdue it. . . "' (*Gen.* 1:27–28).

The continuance of the human race depends for its effectiveness on God's initial blessing, which also gave man authority to subdue the earth and rule over the animal kingdom. That sway was meant to be beneficial. And because man was made in the image of God, all human life, at whatever stage in its development, is sacred and is to be treated accordingly. The divine blessings recorded in Genesis 1 guaranteed the continuance of life on this planet to the end of time. Life did not emerge spontaneously as many scientists would have us believe: God is the source and sustainer of all life.

Material prosperity may also be a divine blessing. We read that 'the LORD blessed the Egyptian's house for Joseph's sake; the blessing of the LORD was on all that he had, in house and field' (*Gen.* 39:5). If the Israelites were obedient to God, they could claim the promise, 'Blessed shall be your basket and your kneading bowl' (*Deut.* 28:5). God bestows 'every good and every perfect gift' (*James* 1:17). In this chapter we shall concentrate on the spiritual blessings enjoyed by the people of God.

THE BLESSING OF FORGIVENESS

Words cannot adequately describe the magnitude of the blessing experienced when sins are forgiven. Sin has resulted in separation between God and man (*Isa.* 59:2). From man's side, there is an unbridgeable gulf between him and God, a yawning chasm of alienation. God hides his face from him (*Isa.* 59:2). He is 'of purer eyes than to see evil and cannot look at wrong' (*Hab.* 1:13). How, then, could man be forgiven?

The message of the Bible is that God in matchless grace took the initiative to bring the forgiveness of sins to all who believe in Jesus Christ. That message is 'good news' indeed. It declares that Christ bore the full penalty of sin when he suffered and died on the cross. For all who trust in him, and in him alone for salvation, there is forgiveness. Nothing could be more radical, far-reaching, complete, and permanent than this divinely provided forgiveness.

God, in his Word, repeatedly emphasizes the absolute and enduring nature of his forgiveness of sin. 'I, I am he who blots out your transgressions for my own sake, and I will not remember your sins' (*Isa.* 43:25). Sin is a blot on the human character and God in grace blots out sin when he forgives the believer.

So David could pray, under the burden of the guilt of his heinous sins of adultery and murder: 'Have mercy on me, O God, according to your steadfast love; according to your abundant mercy blot out my transgressions' (*Psa.* 51:1).

The prophet Micah could also say: 'Who is a God like you, pardoning iniquity . . . He will tread our iniquities underfoot. You will cast all our sins into the depths of the sea' (*Mic.* 7:18–19).

The Lutheran commentator, Theodore Laetsch, observes:

> Our debts, our manifold guilt, which we daily amass by sins of commission and omission, which disturb the believer's peace, our conscience, all these sins He tramples underfoot. They have no right to disturb the peace of those He calls His own. . . And, therefore, as often as sin raises its accusing voice against a child of God, so often does the Lord take that sin, hurl it to the ground, and trample it underfoot. And if, in spite of being ground into the dust, our sin continues to shriek out its accusations against us . . . the Lord takes that sin and casts it into the depths of the sea. The God who has determined to forgive the sins of His children, who has forgotten them so thoroughly as to wipe them out of His

memory, does not want His children to be disturbed by any accusation . . . Who is a God like unto our God?[1]

Sin forgotten, trampled underfoot, cast into the depths of the sea! What could be more thoroughgoing or exhaustive? And note well, it is into 'the depths of the sea' that God casts our sins, not near the shore where the tide might wash them in. This figure of speech is apt in stressing the unequivocal and perpetual nature of God's forgiveness of sin. There are no half-measures with God. God forgets our sins: we cannot forget. But if we allow the memory of our sins to haunt us and rob us of our peace, we dishonour God and undervalue his Word.

There are those who speak of what they term our need to forgive ourselves. From where did that idea originate and how should we respond to it? It stems from the humanistic philosophy of men like Nietzsche and Freud, made popular in theological circles by Harry Emerson Fosdick and Norman Vincent Peale, and, to a lesser extent, more recently by R. T. Kendall. The idea of guilt is seen as something negative. Fosdick maintained that 'integration' ought to replace the word 'salvation'. What matters, in this view, is self-realization. Peale stated that 'the greatest day in any individual's life is when he begins for the first time to realize himself.'[2] All is made to hinge on self-discovery and self-development. The 'new birth' is seen as the integration of one's personality. The real

[1] Theodore Laetsch, *The Minor Prophets* (Saint Louis: Concordia Publishing House, 1956), p. 291.
[2] From *The Art of Living*, quoted by Carl F. H. Henry, *op.cit.*, vol. 4, p. 518.

nature of sin and its consequences, the horrendous chasm that exists between fallen man and a holy God, are not given prominence. 'Learn to forgive yourself', becomes the message, but this concept is not found in the Bible. It is the very antithesis of biblical teaching, which is that 'our old self was crucified' with Christ, and that if we are to follow him we must 'deny' ourselves (*Rom.* 6:6; *Matt.* 16:24). Christian discipleship involves the obliteration of all self-centred, self-promoting thinking.

To speak of forgiving oneself is like dropping the anchor inside the ship instead of on the bed of the ocean. It is a process of self-deception. A holy God turns his back on sin; but when, by his grace, a sinner trusts in Christ as Saviour and Lord, God casts those sins behind his back (*Isa.* 38:17). The believer's sins will be for ever out of God's sight.

The Psalmist confessed: 'But with you there is forgiveness that you may be feared' (*Psa.* 130:4). The fruit of forgiveness is a reverence for God the Forgiver.

THE BLESSING OF GOD'S PRESENCE

From earliest times, God assured his people of his presence and made them aware of it. Yet, without a mediator, man is overwhelmed by the divine presence. After the appearance of the angel of the LORD to Manoah, who quickly realized that he was actually in the presence of God, Manoah said: 'We shall surely die for we have seen God' (*Judg.* 13:22). The Angel was none other than Christ himself, revealing himself in a pre-incarnate appearance. At Sinai, God manifested his presence with thunder and flashes of lightning, and the people 'were afraid and trembled, and they stood far off' (*Exod.* 20:18). Later, he said to Moses: 'You cannot see my face, for man shall not see me and live' (*Exod.* 33:20). God was virtually saying to Moses:

> My face is my direct, immediate, intrinsic self. The essential power of God is irresistible; the essential wisdom inscrutable to the creature. The essential holiness of the Almighty and All-wise is insupportable to that which is tainted with guilt. Hence man shall not see him and live.[3]

Without a mediator we cannot savingly know God or rejoice in the thought of his nearness. The Lord Jesus Christ, and he alone, is that Mediator (*1 Tim.* 2:5). Christ's mediation is all-sufficient as, in heaven, on the basis of his finished work, he intercedes for his people. To suggest that he is just the chief mediator and that assistant mediators are required is a gross dishonour to the Name and priestly office of Jesus Christ.

God's presence with his people now, though invisible, is none the less real. To ancient pagans such an idea was incomprehensible: they needed the tangible. Idolatrous systems still tend in that direction. The Roman General, Pompey, was completely bewildered when, in the first century BC, he entered the Holy of Holies in the Temple at Jerusalem and found no visible representation of God's special presence: long before, the Ark of the Covenant, which did have that symbolism, had been lost. However,

---

[3] J. G. Murphy, *Commentary on the Book of Exodus* (Minneapolis: Klock & Klock Publishers, 1979 reprint), p. 356.

God's real presence in the midst of his people never depended on material symbols.

God often reminded his servants of his presence, especially in times of testing. When he commissioned Moses to go to Pharaoh and demand the release of the Israelites, God said to him, 'I will be with you' (*Exod.* 3:12). After the death of Moses, when Joshua undertook the daunting task of leading Israel into the hostile territory of Canaan, God said to him: 'Just as I was with Moses, so I will be with you' (*Josh.* 1:5).

As the young prophet Samuel grew up, we read that 'the LORD was with him' (*1 Sam.* 3:19). To Isaiah God said: 'Fear not, for I am with you' (*Isa.* 41:10).

When the youthful Jeremiah, whom God had appointed a prophet, pleaded the inexperience of his tender years, God said to him: 'Do not be afraid. . . for I am with you' (*Jer.* 1:8).

When Jonah tried to escape from 'the presence of the LORD' (*Jon.* 1:3), God brought heavy chastisement upon him; but in the belly of the great fish, Jonah did what he failed to do in the ship: He 'called out to the LORD' (*Jon.* 2:2). When anyone prays as Jonah did then, that person is in the presence of God.

When Paul faced danger in Corinth, God said to him, 'Do not be afraid . . . for I am with you' (*Acts* 18:10). We shall later consider these wonderful assurances of God's presence in another context, but for now let us see in them the comforting truth that our sovereign God is always with us. When the Saviour commissioned his church to take the gospel to the whole world, he said: 'I am with you always, to the end of the age' (*Matt.* 28:20): not, 'I will be with you', but 'I *am* with you', and the 'I' is emphatic. Leon Morris comments:

> This Gospel [of Matthew] opened with the assurance that in the coming of Jesus God was with his people (1:23), and it closes with the promise that the very presence of Jesus Christ will never be lacking to his faithful follower.[4]

Christ's promise stands: 'For where two or three are gathered together in my name, there am I among them' (*Matt.* 18:20).

How do we experience the presence of God? When we earnestly pray, he is listening to us. When we meet with his people to worship him, we are in his presence, and should not our conduct and appearance reflect an awareness of this astounding fact? When we meet for worship, we are not paying homage to an earthly king or president. We have come to praise and adore the Lord God Almighty. Can there be any greater or nobler human activity? 'Guard your steps when you go into the house of God' (*Eccles.* 5:1).

Our experience of God's gracious presence now is a foretaste of the unspeakable blessedness that awaits us in heaven; then it will be true as never before that in God's presence there is 'fullness of joy' (*Psa.* 16:11). In heaven we shall see the glory of God in the face of Jesus Christ (2 *Cor.* 4:6), who is the true image of God (2 *Cor.* 4:4).

---

[4] Leon Morris, *Matthew*, p. 749 f.

THE BLESSING OF CHRISTIAN SERVICE

It is not trite to say that we are 'saved to serve'. Without service to God and to others through evangelism and Christian compassion, the Christian's life would soon become self-centred and introverted. James Montgomery Boice comments: 'In God's eyes, greatness consists not in the number of people who serve us but in the number of people we serve. The greater that number, the better the Christian.'[5]

First of all, consider our service to the Lord. Paul reminded the Thessalonian believers that they had 'turned to God from idols to serve the living and true God' (*1 Thess.* 1:9). Becoming a Christian ought not to be seen as something negative; on the contrary, we are 'to serve the living and true God'. Previously we had served the idols on which man's sinful heart dotes. But they are false gods and unreal. The God we now serve is living and true. Can there be a greater privilege or blessing than to serve this sovereign God? After his conversion, Paul served God with his spirit 'in the gospel of his Son' (*Rom.* 1:9). The expression 'in my spirit' indicates the sincerity of his service of God. Christian service, to be worthy of the name, must be wholehearted. There are many ways in which personal and informal Christian service can take place. The Christ-like life is itself a shining testimony to the grace of God.

There are also more formal kinds of service, such as that undertaken by the Christian pastor, missionary, or

---

[5] James Montgomery Boice, *op.cit.*, pp. 630–1.

teacher. But in many occupations there are unique opportunities for witness. However there is a need for balance: there must be increasing maturity in the service of the Lord. Zeal must be matched by humility and compassion. When I entered the ministry, my over-riding passion was to preach the gospel. I never lost that passion. There was, however, a serious lack in my Christian service: I did not really see myself as a 'pastor'. Visits had to be made; the sick had to be seen and prayed for. These tasks I performed as a duty. However, one day I listened to an interview on the radio with an Irish priest who worked on a small island off the west coast of Ireland. He was a distinguished academic. When asked by the interviewer why a man of his intellectual ability should spend his days among some shepherds and fishermen on a small island, he promptly replied: 'I have the care of souls, what could be more important than that? Are not people precious?' I was immediately convicted with a sense of guilt and shame. Here was a man whose religion I could not accept as being true to the Bible, and yet he had an insight that I lacked. He saw himself as a pastor to these people and sought their spiritual well-being. Then and there, by God's grace I resolved to see people as precious and pray for a pastor's heart. That proved a great blessing for me in the coming years, and I trust for others also.

The scope for Christian service is boundless. The whole world is a mission field. John Wesley saw the world as his parish. We need that kind of vision. Many years ago, Harvie Conn of Westminster Theological Seminary said to me: 'You should serve Christ wherever in the church and wherever on the earth you can make the best use of the talents God has given you.' That was good advice.

Paul and Timothy, in the salutation in their Epistle to the Philippians, described themselves as 'servants', literally 'slaves', of Christ Jesus (*Phil.* 1:1). One man was an apostle, the other an evangelist. Timothy has been termed Paul's 'spiritual child', converted through Paul's ministry. Yet in Christ they were equals, both bondservants of Christ.

That term 'slave' is applied to Christians in several places in the New Testament, (cf. *Rom.* 1:1; *1 Cor.* 7:22; *Gal.* 1:10; *Tit.* 1:1). All who serve Christ should do so unconditionally: he has full right of possession: we belong to him.

Referring to the manner in which Paul and Timothy introduced themselves, Jac J. Müller writes:

> This lowly and humble self-appellation, . . . is a renunciation of all self-importance and self-esteem, and so the light is focused more intensely on Him Who alone is their Lord, 'to Whom they belong and Whom they serve'.[6]

Would that more preachers and evangelists would follow their example! George Whitefield preached the gospel with zeal and passion and saw God using his ministry in a wonderful way. Yet after some thirty years of preaching, Whitefield prayed, 'Lord help me to begin to begin.'

---

[6] Jac J. Müller, *The Epistle of Paul to the Philippians and to Philemon* (London: Marshall, Morgan & Scott, 1955), p. 34.

It is interesting that in certain passages in the Old Testament where God refers to Abraham, Moses, and Joshua as his servants, the Septuagint, the Greek translation of the Old Testament, uses the same Greek word for slave, *doulos* (*Josh.* 24:29; *Psa.* 105:6; *Mal.* 4:4). We are at our Sovereign Lord's disposal; he is the best of masters and serving him in loving obedience is a real blessing.

The need and the opportunities for serving the Lord are great. We can make the gospel known through preaching the Word, Christian literature, and personal witness. The church's mission cannot fail. God says of his spoken Word, '. . . it shall not return to me empty, but it shall accomplish that which I purpose and shall succeed in the thing for which I sent it' (*Isa.* 55:11).

The Hebrew poets and prophets had the vision of multitudes worldwide being brought into the kingdom of God. They expressed themselves in types and symbols. Thinking of a great spiritual renewal, Isaiah wrote: 'This one will say, "I am the LORD's", another will call on the name of Jacob, and another will write on his hand, "The LORD's", and name himself by the name of Israel' (*Isa.* 44:5). In Psalm 87 the triumph of the gospel throughout the world is envisaged in a similar manner. There we read about 'Zion'. To the Jews, Zion was much more than an ancient, earthly city. In Zion the temple stood, and there God dwelt amongst his people: this must be remembered when we read and sing the Psalms. So in Psalm 87 we read of those who will come to know the Lord: Rahab (Egypt), Babylon, Philistia, Tyre, and Cush (Ethiopia); all ancient enemies of Israel and Israel's God, now seen as one with his chosen and redeemed people. 'Glorious things' are spoken of the 'city of God' which will embrace citizens from every land and every age.

It is important to recognize the role of symbolism in the Old Testament. It belongs to the warp and woof of Hebrew thought and expression. Alfred Edersheim, with his valuable insights as a believing Jew, writes of

> the place occupied by symbolism, not only in the Old Testament, but in Hebrew, and in a measure in all Eastern thinking. Symbolism is, so to speak, its mode of expression – the language of its highest thinking. Hence its moral teaching is in parables and proverbs; its dogmatics in ritual and typical institutions: while in its prophecy the present serves as a mirror in which the future is reflected.[7]

A glorious future for the kingdom of God through the power of his Word was a dominant thought in the minds of Israel's greatest teachers. That was no idle dream as history shows. Napoleon Bonaparte exclaimed:

> Everything in Jesus astonishes me. Alexander, Charlemagne and myself founded empires; but upon what did we rest the creation of our genius? Upon force! Jesus Christ alone founded his empire upon love; and at this hour, millions of men would die for him.

He was right: millions have suffered and died for him. In heaven we shall be part of a great multitude that no one can number, gathered from every nation, tribe,

---

[7] Alfred Edersheim, *Old Testament History*, p. 898

people, and language, which shall stand before the throne and the Lamb (*Rev.* 7:9). Then we shall know that in the Lord 'our labour was not in vain' (*1 Cor.* 15:58).

When we wholeheartedly serve the Lord, we will also serve one another in love. Indeed we are commanded to do so: ' . . . through love serve one another' (*Gal.* 5:13). The one service results from the other.

In the book of Acts we read of how the believers 'had all things in common. And they were selling their possessions and belongings and distributing the proceeds to all, as any had need.' They had 'glad and generous hearts' (*Acts* 2:44–46). They were concerned to meet the needs of others. Just like them, we are to 'bear one another's burdens, and so fulfil the law of Christ' (*Gal.* 6:2). 'Love is the fulfilling of the law' (*Rom.* 13:10). When asked what was 'the great commandment of the Law', Christ replied:

> You shall love the Lord your God with all your heart and with all your soul and with all your mind. This is the great and first commandment. And a second is like it: You shall love your neighbour as yourself. On these two commandments depend all the Law and the Prophets (*Matt.* 22:37–40; cf. *Deut.* 6:4; *Lev.* 19:18, 34).

Thinking of love as the fulfilling of the law, Herman Ridderbos says: 'There is here a double commandment, but no double love.'[8]

Love for God shows itself in all human relationships: it is all pervading. No Christian, then, should be left to

---

[8] Herman Ridderbos, *Paul*, p. 299.

shoulder a burden alone.[9] 'So then, as we have opportunity, let us do good to everyone, and especially to those who are of the household of faith' (*Gal.* 6:10).

All Christian service, without exception, is rendered to God. Calvin saw this clearly when he wrote: 'To serve God is the purpose for which we have been born, and for which we are preserved in life.'[10] And again: 'I call "service" not only what lies in obedience to God's Word, but what turns the mind of man, empty of its own carnal sense, wholly to the bidding of God's Spirit.'[11]

THE BLESSING OF CHRISTIAN FELLOWSHIP

The word used in the New Testament for fellowship, *koinonia*, means to share. It can refer to practical assistance (*Rom.* 15:26), sharing in Christian witness (*Phil.* 1:5) and spiritual fellowship (*1 Cor.* 10:16).

Believers have fellowship with Christ. God has called them 'into the fellowship of his Son, Jesus Christ our Lord' (*1 Cor.* 1:9). These words indicate something inward and present.

Believers participate in the life of Christ because of their close union with him. There is a sense in which Christians share (fellowship) Christ's sufferings (*Phil.* 3:10). This fellowship also results from union with Christ. As we share

---

[9] The statement in Galatians 6:5, 'Each will have to bear his own load', considered in context, means that one is accountable to God for one's thoughts and actions. That burden cannot be shared; cf. *Rom.* 14:12.

[10] John Calvin, *Commentary on the Psalms* (*Psa.* 111:10).

[11] *Institutes*, III:7:1.

the life of the risen Saviour, so also we share his sufferings. This does not mean sharing in Christ's redemptive suffering, which was completed on the cross. Rather, it means the crucifying of the flesh (*Gal.* 5:24) and suffering for Christ's sake (*Matt.* 5:11–12). Living for Christ in an unbelieving and hostile world makes suffering inevitable for the Christian.

Christian fellowship is produced by the Holy Spirit. It is 'of the Holy Spirit' (2 *Cor.* 13:14). This bond that we have with Christ and through him with other believers transcends all other relationships. It is a fellowship that is both inclusive and exclusive: 'What fellowship has light with darkness? What accord has Christ with Belial? Or what portion does a believer share with an unbeliever?' (2 *Cor.* 6:14–16). It is impossible for the believer to experience Christian fellowship with unbelievers.

Christian fellowship is unhampered by material, racial or cultural barriers, or denominational differences. When Christian meets Christian there is an instant bond in the faith, for we are 'all one in Christ Jesus' (*Gal.* 3:28). When two or more Christians discuss and treasure the doctrines of the gospel of grace, there is true fellowship. When they share Christian experiences, study God's Word together, or pray together, there is fellowship. Friendly conversation is pleasant, but Christian fellowship is richer and deeper. In times of testing and trial, Christian fellowship is a great comfort. In Malachi 3:16 we read: 'Then those who feared the LORD spoke with one another. The LORD paid attention and heard them, and a book of remembrance was written before him of those who feared the LORD and esteemed his name.' Such fellowship strengthens believers, preserves the truth, witnesses against unfaithfulness, and is honoured by God. It will be increasingly manifested in one's life: 'If we walk in the light as he [God] is in the light, we have fellowship with one another, and the blood of Jesus his Son cleanses from all sin' (*1 John* 1:7). Truly the blessings God bestows are 'more than can be numbered' (*Psa.* 40:5, KJV).

The Bible speaks of blessing and curse. As the essentially holy One, God is not indifferent to sin. Therefore the alternative to salvation is condemnation (*John* 3:18). Our Lord taught that when a person dies, his soul goes to either heaven or hell (*Luke* 16:19–26). Reader, if you are not a Christian, you know nothing of the blessing of forgiveness. Moses presented the crucial alternatives to Israel:

> See, I am setting before you today a blessing and a curse: the blessing, if you obey the commandments of the LORD your God, which I command you today, and the curse if you do not obey the commandments of the LORD your God, but turn aside from the way I am commanding you today (*Deut.* 11:26–27).

Joshua presented the same choice to them: 'Choose this day whom you will serve . . . But as for me and my house, we will serve the LORD' (*Josh.* 24:15). The same choice confronts you now. On this matter of your eternal welfare, there can be no neutrality. You must choose.

> I call heaven and earth to witness against you today, that I have set before you life and death, blessing and curse.

Therefore choose life, that you and your offspring may live, loving the LORD your God, obeying his voice and holding fast to him (*Deut.* 30:19–20).

I urge you, choose life!

9

THE HAND THAT ENABLES

On 17 April 1521, Martin Luther appeared before the Diet of Worms to account for the books he had written, all twenty-five of them being laid before him on a table. The Diet before which the young monk stood was an august assembly: the Emperor, Papal legates, archbishops, bishops, princes, ambassadors, and an array of dignitaries of varying rank. When asked about his books, Luther's voice was barely audible. He was clearly overcome by the ordeal of facing the highest powers in Church and State. Those closest to him thought he was about to collapse. Luther asked for further time to consider his position and was granted one more day.

That night, Luther spent time in prayer and meditation. Next day a very different Luther stood before the Diet. He was rock firm and spoke in a clear voice that all could hear. When pressed to recant by his interrogator, Dr Eck, Luther replied: 'Here I stand. I cannot do otherwise. God help me! Amen'.[1] His prayer for God's help had been answered. Well does Philip Schaff say of Luther: 'He

---

[1] There is a difference of opinion, among historians, as to the precise words used by Luther on this occasion, but the statement just given is essentially what he said.

stood there as the fearless champion of the supremacy of the word of God over the traditions of men, and of the liberty of conscience over the tyranny of authority.'[2]

It is not enough just to read history. We should think about what we have read and employ all the powers of our God-given imagination. It was an unprecedented event when a lone monk challenged the authority of the Papacy and denied the infallibility of Church Councils; and in the providence of God, it became one of those world-changing moments of lasting significance. The 'hand of God' was upon Luther that day: he was made strong in the Lord.

He was not the first to know that strength: Scripture provides many examples.

CALL AND COMMISSION

In Scripture we see how our sovereign God calls and commissions his servants. His call can come unexpectedly. God called Abraham to leave his own country to go to a land that he would show him (*Gen.* 12:1), and Abraham obeyed. He called Moses to lead the Israelites out of Egypt and equipped him for the task. Similarly he called Isaiah, Jeremiah, and Jonah. His call was virtually a command: he had an appointed mission for each one of them to accomplish.

The Lord Jesus, God incarnate, also issued calls and commissions. To Simon and Andrew, two busy fishermen, he said, 'Follow me, and I will make you become fishers

[2] Philip Schaff, *History of the Christian Church* (Grand Rapids: Wm. B. Eerdmans 1960), Vol.7, p.311.

of men.' Then he saw James and John mending their nets and he repeated the call to them (*Mark*: 1:17, 19–20). He saw Matthew, a tax collector, sitting at his desk, and said to him, 'Follow me' (*Matt.* 9:9). In each case this call to follow Christ implied discipleship, the breaking of all other ties to follow Christ exclusively and forever.

When the risen Saviour encountered Saul of Tarsus near Damascus, revealing himself to the zealous bigot as the Jesus whom he was persecuting, he told him to enter the city where he would be told what to do. Then the Lord commanded Ananias to go and find Saul. Understandably, Ananias was fearful of meeting this ferocious persecutor. But the Lord said to him:

> Go, for he is a chosen instrument of mine to carry my name before the Gentiles and kings and the children of Israel. For I will show him how much he must suffer for the sake of my name' (*Acts* 9:6, 13–16).

In spite of his record as a persecutor of Christians, Paul was God's chosen messenger to proclaim the good news throughout the world, to Jew and Gentile alike. He had made others suffer for Christ's sake; now it was ordained that he must also suffer in this way. Paul was profoundly aware of the fact that God had a design for his life even before he was born. Probably with Jeremiah 1:5 in mind, he wrote of God setting him apart before he was born (*Gal.* 1:15); that is, of being set apart for a special purpose, of being chosen and appointed. From the moment of his conception, God was forming his personality and temperament to suit his life's work. God does not call and commission many who possess the intellectual gifts of Paul. As he himself later wrote to the Corinthian believers, '. . . not many of you were wise according to worldly standards, not many were powerful, not many were of noble birth' (*1 Cor.* 1:26).

> This is His will: He takes and He refuses,
> Finds Him ambassadors whom men deny,
> Wise ones nor mighty for His saints He chooses,
> No, such as John or Gideon or I.
> *Frederic W. H. Myers*

When God calls he enables. All his people have been called by him and to him. The word translated 'church' in the New Testament refers to the assembly of those who have been 'called out', *ekklesia*. In the Septuagint the term *ekklesia* is used of the congregation of God's people, (cf. *Psa.* 137:32; *Prov.* 5:14). God repeatedly reminded Israel that he had called them (*Isa.* 41:9; 48:12; 51:2). We have a similar reminder of our call in the New Testament. We are 'called to be saints' (*1 Cor.* 1:2), 'called to freedom' (*Gal.* 5:13), called to 'eternal life' (*1 Tim.* 6:12, cf. *Rom.* 8:28; 9:11; *2 Thess.* 2:13–14).

God's call and God's choice are linked: he calls whom he has chosen. David could say that God chose him and appointed him a 'prince over Israel' (*2 Sam.* 6:21). To the people of Israel he said, '. . . the LORD God of Israel chose me from all my father's house to be king over Israel for ever. For he chose Judah as leader, and in the house of Judah my father's house, and among my father's sons he took pleasure in me to make me king over all Israel. And of all my sons . . . he has chosen Solomon . . . to sit on the throne of the kingdom of the LORD over Israel (*1 Chron.* 28:4–5). God had said to David concerning Solomon: 'I have chosen him to be my son . . . I will establish his kingdom . . .' (*1 Chron.* 28:6–7).

God's choice and call are sovereign acts. He chooses whom he will, and always with an end in view. He calls and he uses for his glory those whom he has called. This is a very comforting truth. When one senses the call of God to some particular service and the call is confirmed by providence and by the church, one has the assurance that this call did not originate in one's own mind, but that its author is God. In all Christian service of this kind, be it that of elder, pastor, teacher, or missionary, it is crucial that this sense of calling is paramount. There are times when the Christian worker may feel like abandoning the work altogether, because of discouragements and apparent failure. What keeps him on course at such a time is the awareness of God's call. Tearfully, he may at times pray: 'Did you call me, Lord?', but in his heart he knows the answer. Never let the reality of that call fade: Moses, Jeremiah, David, Paul, never doubted their call or the commission that accompanied it.

HESITANT RESPONSE

The biblical examples of God calling and commissioning are impressive and repay careful study. One of the most thought provoking is the call of Moses. Standing before the burning bush, Moses heard the call of God. God spoke to him as the covenant-keeping God, 'the God of your father, the God of Abraham, the God of Isaac and the God of Jacob' (*Exod.* 3:6). 'And God heard their groaning, and God remembered his covenant with Abraham, with Isaac, and with Jacob. God saw the people of Israel – and God knew' (*Exod.* 2:24–25). He had seen the affliction of his people in Egypt and heard their cry. Then God said to Moses: 'Come, I will send you to Pharaoh that you may bring my people, the children of Israel, out of Egypt' (*Exod.* 3:10). Moses was called and commissioned.

What thoughts must have gone through his mind at that moment! He had been raised as the adopted son of Pharaoh's daughter. He had been a prince in Pharaoh's palace, 'instructed in all the wisdom of the Egyptians . . . mighty in words and deeds' (*Acts* 7:22). As a prince, he probably had led a military expedition, common practice for such men. (A BBC interviewer once asked General Montgomery whom he considered to be the greatest general of all time. His reply was not the one the reporter expected to hear: 'Moses'!)

Moses must have remembered how he had killed an Egyptian who was beating a Hebrew, 'one of his people' (*Exod.* 3:11), and how, when this became known, he had run for his life.

Forty years had passed since then. Probably, if he returned, most of the people would have forgotten all about him. But would this have been the case at the palace? The prince who had suddenly run away for helping a Hebrew slave would not be forgotten there. Oh, the prospect of entering the royal precincts and standing before the king of one of the greatest nations on earth, must have made Moses quake with fear.

There is, however, another side to this story. During those forty years as a shepherd in the land of Midian, Moses had matured spiritually, his character had ripened, and he had experienced life in the Arabian desert, all of which were vital for his future work. Doubtless the spiritual teaching he had received in childhood from his natural mother came back to him. Now God's call and commission struck a chord. In his heart he sympathized with the suffering Israelites: for was he not one of them? Moses 'refused to be called the son of Pharaoh's daughter, choosing rather to be mistreated with the people of God than to enjoy the fleeting pleasures of sin. He considered the reproach of Christ greater wealth than the treasures of Egypt' (*Heb.* 11:24–26). As Joseph was God's man to preserve Israel in Egypt, so Moses was God's man to lead them out from Egypt.

Now, as Moses heard God speak, he asked himself, 'Am I the right person to undertake so daunting a task?' He began to express his doubts and fears. 'Who am I that I should go to Pharaoh and bring the children of Israel out of Egypt' (*Exod.* 3:11). He was really asking, 'What qualifications do I possess for such a momentous undertaking? And should I go, who shall I say has sent me? When the people ask, "What is his name?", what shall I tell them? (*Exod.* 3:13). What happens if they do not believe me? Besides, I am not eloquent enough to stand before Pharaoh and his courtiers and address them.' One by one, God allayed his fears. But Moses still held back:

'Oh, my Lord, please send someone else' (*Exod.* 4:13). God's anger was kindled, yet he was patient with his fearful servant. Aaron, Moses' brother, would be his spokesman. God would instruct Moses and Moses in turn would instruct Aaron: 'You shall be as God to him' (*Exod.* 4:16). God accompanied his word to Moses with supernatural signs.

Moses is often depicted as an unwilling servant who made all these excuses. True, left to himself, this task was the last thing he (or anyone else for that matter!) would wish to undertake. But does that mean that Moses was unwilling to obey God? Would Paul have wanted to be imprisoned, receive repeated beatings, be 'often near death', stoned, shipwrecked; to have sleepless nights, and be hungry and thirsty? (2 *Cor.* 11:23–27). Would the prospect of such an experience have appealed to his human nature? Certainly not. But that does not mean that he was unwilling to serve his Lord, which he did unflinchingly. We shall come back to consider Moses' attitude after we have looked at another similar case.

God told Jeremiah that he was chosen to be a prophet. 'Before I formed you in the womb I knew you, and before you were born I consecrated you; I appointed you a prophet to the nations' (*Jer.* 1:5). What a profound statement! God formed him in the womb. The Psalmist too could say: 'For you formed my inward parts, you knitted me together in my mother's womb . . .' (*Psa.* 139:13–16). Before time began, God 'knew', God 'loved' Jeremiah. In grace God consecrated or sanctified him, setting him apart for service. God appointed him to the prophetic office before his mother conceived him. He gave Jeremiah the character, temperament and talents that would qualify him for this high office he was to fulfil. Those who do not believe in predestination would do well to ponder these words of God to his prophet.

Jeremiah was clearly taken aback by this word from the Lord. How could he ever be a prophet? The days were evil. Idolatry and disregard for God's law were commonplace. It would take immense courage to be a prophet at such a time. And so Jeremiah began to express his fears. 'Ah, Lord GOD! Behold, I do not know how to speak, for I am only a youth' (*Jer.* 1:6). He was saying: 'I lack experience, and am not gifted to preach. How could someone like me meet the challenge of this hour?' Like Moses, he was called and commissioned by God, but he shuddered at the thought of being a prophet of the Lord. He felt unworthy and incompetent for such an office. Are we to regard such timidity as unwillingness to serve God? Were Moses and Jeremiah simply making excuses, or were they sincerely expressing their fears and their feelings of inadequacy? Both men did serve the Lord valiantly and at great personal cost.

The false prophets knew no such reluctance. God says of them: 'I did not send the prophets, yet they ran; I did not speak to them, yet they prophesied' (*Jer.* 23:21). There are those who are overly keen to preach and who display an overweening self-confidence that ill becomes the true ambassadors of Christ.

It must not be thought that when we sense the call of God, we are to try to be modern-day Jeremiahs or react in the same way as Moses. There is no indication that Abraham hesitated when God called him. And Isaiah was prompt to respond when he heard God say, 'Whom shall I send, and who will go for us?' (*Isa.* 6:8).

> 'Here am I! Send me' (verse 8), replied Isaiah. It is a joyous response. He doesn't regard service as a sacrifice or a burden. He doesn't consider that he is doing God a favour by agreeing to be his messenger. On the contrary, he can hardly believe that such a privilege is being offered to him . . . That the great God chooses to use him creates not a sinking feeling of obligation but a delighted shout of praise . . . His commitment is unconditional . . . 'Here am I! Send me' – anywhere! – for anything![3]

There is not a vestige of self-confidence in Isaiah's response to God's call. He had just undergone a radical change in God's presence when, in true repentance, he was granted forgiveness. One of the seraphim touched his mouth with a burning coal taken from God's altar, and said: 'Behold, this has touched your lips; your guilt is taken away, and your sin atoned for' (*Isa.* 6:6–7). As a result of that experience, he was now an instrument far more fit for service than he could ever have been otherwise.

ASSURANCE GIVEN

When those whom God has called hesitate in fear, God always brought reassurance to them. To Moses he said: 'I

[3] Edward Donnelly, 'The Reformed Faith – What Is It?', *The Banner of Truth,* May 2005, pp. 5–6.

will be with you.' When Moses wanted to know what name he could use when meeting the Israelites, God spoke to him in the language of the covenant. God said to him: 'I am the God of your father, the God of Abraham, the God of Isaac, and the God of Jacob.' When God heard the cry of his people in Egypt, he 'remembered his covenant' with the patriarchs, the covenant of grace confirmed with them. And so he told Moses to say to the Israelites, 'I AM has sent me to you' (*Exod.* 3:14), the covenant God of their fathers.

The names of God grew in number as he revealed himself to his people, e.g., *Elohim*, the Majestic One; *El Shaddai*, the Almighty God. God now uses the name *Yahweh*, 'I AM'. Yahweh probably means 'He is', that is, the self-existing God, the unchanging God. That divine name occurs frequently in the original Hebrew of the book of Genesis: 12:1, 7, 8; 14:22; 15:2, 6; 17:1; 18:26; 21:33; 22:14; 25:21; 28:13, 16, 21.

Yet God said to Moses: 'I appeared to Abraham, to Isaac, and to Jacob, as God Almighty, but by my name the LORD [*Yahweh*] I did not make myself known to them' (*Exod.* 6:3). The biblical references above show that the name Yahweh was not unknown to the patriarchs, but there is no contradiction here. J. G. Murphy comments helpfully that previously God (*Yahweh*) was known 'only as a promiser, not yet as a performer . . . As the performer of promise, the giver of existence to that purpose which he had expressed, he was not known, personally and practically known, to them.'[4] Geerhardus Vos concurs

---

[4] J. G. Murphy, *Exodus*, p. 64

with this view: 'The statement [*Exod.*6:3] need mean nothing more than that the patriarchs did not as yet possess the practical knowledge and experience of that side of the divine character which finds expression in the name [Yahweh].'[5] It is also true to say that while this name of God was previously well known, now for the first time its *meaning* was fully known. Other 'names' for God were really descriptive (e.g., majestic, almighty etc.): this was the only genuinely divine name.

Now God was about to enable Moses to lead Israel from Egypt to the borders of Canaan: God the 'promiser' was also God the 'performer'. In the immediate context in which God spoke to Moses as I AM, 'it appears that God in his Yahwistic character is the self-existent, self-determining, faithful God of the covenant.'[6] The covenantal aspect of this name was of the utmost importance for Moses' mission. It would

> animate the people with hope and resolution. Moses was now, therefore, armed with a name of potent significance by which to designate him by whose authority he was to approach the people. He could say, he in whose name I come is about to realize the promise of the land of Canaan made to the seed of Abraham; and he has designed to embody this fact in a significant name, indicating his present adherence to his covenant with your fathers.[7]

[5] Geerhardus Vos, *Biblical Theology*, p. 130.
[6] Robert L. Reymond, *Systematic Theology*, p. 158.
[7] J. G. Murphy, *Exodus*, p. 41 f.

God remembered his covenant: good news for Israel! The name *Yahweh* would be a constant reminder to Israel of the covenant faithfulness of their God: it occurs some six thousand times in the Old Testament, reminding God's people of the unchangeableness of God's relationship to them. Christ, who has realized for his people the promises of the covenant of grace, described himself as the I AM, not what he will be, but what he always *is*, the Way, the Truth, the Life, etc.

When God told Joshua, Moses' successor, to lead his people across the Jordan to the promised land, he said:

> No man shall be able to stand before you all the days of your life. Just as I was with Moses, so I will be with you. I will not leave you or forsake you . . . Be strong and courageous. Do not be frightened and do not be dismayed, for the LORD your God is with you wherever you go (*Josh.* 1:5, 9).

How often in the Bible do we hear God saying to his people: 'Fear not' or 'Do not be afraid'! This he said to Abraham, Hagar, Isaac, Jacob, Israel (repeatedly through her prophets, e.g., *Isa.* 41:14), Jeremiah, Ezekiel, Daniel, and in the New Testament by his angel to Joseph, Zechariah, Mary, and to the shepherds of Bethlehem. The Lord Jesus said 'Fear not' to his disciples, Simon, Jairus, Paul, and to John on Patmos: and such examples could be further multiplied! No wonder Amy Carmichael asks why God's people are ever afraid and speaks of 'the reiterated *Fear not*'. Yet in our present imperfection we all are afraid at times. How we need to listen to God's comforting word!

POWER DISPLAYED

The word 'hand' is often used to convey the idea of action. A father may ask his son, 'Could you give me a hand in the garden?', or a mother may say to her daughter, 'Can you give me a hand in the kitchen?'

When we read of God's hand in the Bible we are to think of his invincible sovereignty in action. The touch of his hand empowers and enables, or else crushes and overthrows. When after a time of severe drought, Elijah confronted the idolatrous Ahab to announce that heavy rain was about to fall, 'the hand of the LORD was on Elijah' (*1 Kings* 18:46).

When in a similar situation, Elisha said to Jehoram, the wicked son of Ahab, that God would send rain and grant victory to Israel in battle, 'the hand of the LORD came upon him' (*2 Kings* 3:15).

When Nehemiah approached the Persian monarch asking that he be allowed to rebuild Jerusalem, it pleased the king to accede to his request. And Nehemiah wrote: 'And the king granted me what I asked, for the good hand of my God was upon me' (*Neh.* 2:8; cf. 2:18).

While Ezekiel the priest was an exile in Babylon, the 'word of the LORD' came to him and he was called to discharge the functions of a prophet, and we read that 'the hand of the LORD was upon him there' (*Ezek.* 1:3).

. . . the Lord, now, by a Divine touch, invigorated his frame and endowed him with strength of eye and elevation of soul for the lofty sphere he was to occupy. And thus raised on high by the immediate agency of God, he was in a condition for witnessing and reporting aright what passed in the region of his inner man.[8]

Calvin writes here:

I take 'hand' to mean divine power, as if Ezekiel had said that he was endued with divine power, so that it should be quite clear that he was chosen a Prophet. The hand of God, then, was a proof of new favour, so that Ezekiel might subject to his own sway all the captives, since he carried with him the authority of God.[9]

In similar fashion, the hand of God touched Daniel to strengthen him (*Dan.* 10:10, 18). In the New Testament, when Elizabeth the wife of Zechariah the priest gave birth to a son, the father who had been unable to speak since receiving the heavenly message that a son would be born to him, suddenly spoke saying, 'His name is John', in accordance with the angel's instructions. 'For the hand of the Lord was with him' (*Luke* 1:66).

When on Patmos, John heard a voice commanding him to write, he saw the risen, glorified Christ and 'fell at his feet as though dead.' John states that the Lord 'laid his right hand on me' and again commanded him to write (*Rev.* 1:11, 17, 19). That touch enabled him to undertake the task of recording the many visions he was to see: he was upheld by the power of God. To encounter the Lord in all his majesty and glory must be an overwhelming experience for mortal man. Compare the experience of

[8] Patrick Fairbairn, *An Exposition of Ezekiel* (Minneapolis: Klock & Klock Publishers, 1979 reprint), p. 26.

[9] John Calvin, *Commentary on the First Twenty Chapters of Ezekiel.*

Ezekiel, Daniel, and Paul (*Ezek.* 1:28; *Dan.* 10:9; *Acts* 9:3–4).

It is abundantly clear from Scripture, that our sovereign God calls and commissions, but it is also as clear that he empowers and equips his servants. Their labour in the Lord is not in vain (*1 Cor.* 15:58). In the book of Acts, we read of 'men of Cyprus and Cyrene' who came to Antioch and spoke to the Greeks, 'preaching the Lord Jesus. And the hand of the Lord was with them, and a great number who believed turned to the Lord' (*Acts* 11:20–21). In times of spiritual awakening and revival, the hand of God is clearly manifest. Prophets and apostles alike had the same commission, to proclaim the word of the Lord. We now have that word complete in Scripture and the same divine commission applies to all the people of God. As God's Word is earnestly and prayerfully made known, the hand of God is stretched out in quickening, transforming, and saving power.

This truth is illustrated in the history of the church since apostolic times in the lives of men like Luther, Calvin, and Tyndale. At the Diet of Worms, Luther stated that his conscience was captive to the Word of God, and therefore he could not recant those teachings that were true to the Word. Later he said: 'I simply taught, preached, wrote God's Word: otherwise I did nothing . . . The Word did it all.' Probably Luther's greatest achievement was his translating the Bible into the common language of the German people; the New Testament which he completed in 1521, and the Old Testament in 1534. While he was translating the Old Testament, his New Testament had appeared in some seventeen editions and more than fifty reprints. The publishers made a fortune, but Luther never made a penny! His sole concern was to place the Bible in the hands of ordinary people, in words that they could easily read. Not only did Luther's German Bible mould and enhance the German language, but under God it made the Reformation in Germany unstoppable.

Johann Cochlaeus, a member of the Diet of Worms and a spokesman for the Papacy, wrote a scathing history of Luther (*Historia Lutheri*) in which he said:

> . . . Luther's New Testament had been so propagated and widely spread by the book printers that even tailors and shoemakers, indeed women and other simple idiots, who had accepted this new Lutheran Gospel – though they could read only a little German – read it eagerly as if it were a fountain of all truth. Some carried it in their bosoms and learned it by heart. Thus they claimed within a few months such skill and experience that without timidity they debated not only with Catholic laymen, but also with priests and monks, indeed with masters and doctors of Sacred Scripture concerning faith and the Gospel. What is more, there were some despicable women who published German books and propositions proudly rejecting the supposed ignorance of men, thereby engaging in debate not only with laymen and other private persons, but also with licentiates, doctors and entire universities . . . [10]

[10] Quoted by H. J. Hillerbrand in *The Reformation in Its Own Words* (London: SCM Press, 1964), pp. 388–9.

Could a greater compliment have been paid to the Reformer?

Calvin, who owed much to Luther, saw himself first and foremost as a preacher of the Word. As an expositor of Scripture he excelled and ranks among the greatest. In 1536, Calvin supervised the revision of Olivétan's French translation of the Bible. 'His labour, with the assistance of Theodore Beza and Louis Budé, finally produced the French 'Geneva Bible', . . . that dominated French-speaking Protestantism for two centuries.'[11]

Calvin encouraged English Protestants, who took refuge in Geneva, to produce an English version of the 'Geneva Bible', translated from the original Hebrew and Greek. It became popular in England in the sixteenth and seventeenth centuries, where it went through more than two hundred printings between 1560 and 1644. This was the version of the Bible that the Pilgrim Fathers took with them when they set sail on the *Mayflower* in 1620, and it was the Bible of the colonial Puritans.

Apart from his extensive correspondence and astounding literary work (amounting to a total of some seventy-one volumes), Calvin preached every other week daily from the Old Testament, and from the New Testament on Sunday mornings and the Psalms on Sunday afternoons.

Calvin's sermons are most beneficial when read aloud. A profitable exercise is for a small group, say three or four, to meet regularly and read aloud one of Calvin's

[11] Robert L. Reymond, *John Calvin: His Life and Influence* (Fearn: Christian Focus Publications, 2004), p. 46.

sermons (some of which are available in good English translations[12]) and then discuss it.

The Geneva to which Calvin came in 1536 was chaotic, crime-ridden, and wicked. The city that Calvin left when he died in 1564 was an orderly society, a 'Christian' city. John Knox called it 'the most perfect school of Christ on earth since the days of the apostles.' How appropriate was the Genevan motto, *Post Tenebras Lux*, 'After Darkness, Light'. What brought about such an amazing transformation? The preaching of the Word by Calvin and the Reformed pastors of Geneva. How we need such preaching today! The weakness of so many pulpits (even Reformed!) is lamentable. Sermons are often limp and dreary. No fire! No passion! No pleading with souls! Much that claims to be evangelical is man-centred, seldom rising above a message of 'See what Jesus can do for you.' As if God existed for the sake of man! What about God's law, God's kingdom, and the lordship of Jesus Christ?

Calvin saw the importance of preaching the Word. He trained many men to take the gospel into his native land of France. The French Calvinists became known as 'Huguenots'. Those taught in the Genevan Academy, including men like Miles Coverdale, John Foxe, and John Knox, helped to spread the Reformed Faith to Scotland, England, much of Europe and ultimately to the New World.

[12] John Calvin's *Sermons on 2 Samuel 1–13*; *Sermons on the Beatitudes*; *Sermons on Galatians*; and *Sermons on Ephesians* are all published by the Banner of Truth Trust. Facsimile editions of his *Sermons on Job*, and *Sermons on Timothy and Titus* are also available from the Trust.

In the sixteenth century William Tyndale translated most of the Bible from the original Hebrew and Greek into English. To a critical cleric Tyndale said: 'If God spare my life, ere many years pass, I will cause a boy that driveth the plough shall know more of the Scriptures than thou dost.' In vain did the English bishops try to ban Tyndale's Bible from the marketplace. Earlier during the fourteenth century, John Wyclif was involved in the translation of the Bible from the Latin into English and copies of it were circulated clandestinely, its message being proclaimed across the country by Wyclif's preachers, the Lollards. But Wyclif's Bible had never been printed. Tyndale's translation was much superior to that of Wyclif because it went straight to the original languages. Tyndale's Bible was immensely influential. The translators of the Authorized or King James Version leaned heavily on his translation: in places the Authorized Version is word-for-word the same as Tyndale.

Both Wyclif and Tyndale were determined to make the Bible accessible to the ordinary people of their day in a homely style, and to see men and women come to a knowledge of the Saviour through the proclamation of its liberating message. They both faced the hostility of Rome. Their sole weapon was spiritual, the Word of God alone – a penetrating two-edged sword and a mighty hammer that crushes the hard rock of unbelief and falsehood. This must be our sole weapon today. This is the weapon God uses. When in times of persecution, Christians have resorted to armed resistance and have become embroiled in politics, their cause has invariably suffered. Christ said: 'My kingdom is not of this world. If my kingdom were of this world, my servants would have been fighting, that I might not be delivered over to the Jews' (*John* 18:36). May we all learn afresh that 'the weapons of our warfare are not of the flesh but have divine power to destroy strongholds' (2 *Cor.* 10:4). In this way alone we shall know the enabling power of God.

THE HAND THAT JUDGES

If you had visited Wigtown, in south-west Scotland, at the end of the seventeenth century, you might have seen an unsmiling, morose old man carrying a large jar full of water, from which he drank constantly. As he approached, people shrank back and children ran to their parents. To begin to understand this grim figure, we need to take a further step back in time.

On 11 May 1685, Margaret Wilson, an eighteen-year-old Covenanter and her elderly friend, Margaret Maclachlan, were tied to stakes on the sands of Wigtown Bay on the Solway Firth at low tide. The older woman was placed some distance in front of Margaret Wilson so that the younger woman could watch her drown. The persecutors hoped that Margaret's will would be broken and she would confess the errors of her ways. To the last Margaret Wilson remained firm. A few words would have been enough to save her life, but she would not attribute to an earthly king that which belonged exclusively to Christ, the only Head of the Church. Before being bound to the stake, she read aloud the eighth chapter of the epistle to the Romans, and then she sang some verses from the twenty-fifth Psalm:

My sins and faults of youth
  do Thou, O Lord, forget:
After Thy mercy think on me,
  and for Thy goodness great.

God good and upright is:
  the way He'll sinners show,
The meek in judgment He will guide,
  and make His path to know.
Scottish Metrical Version

Released from the stake, Margaret was given a last chance to conform. 'I will not', she said, 'I am one of Christ's children, let me go.' At that a man who was the Town Officer of Wigtown, took his halberd and pushed her under the water until she drowned, saying as he did so, 'Tak' anither drink, hinny! And clep wi' the partons' (gossip with the crabs). This was the broken, tormented old man who wandered through the streets of Wigtown, obsessed with swallowing water! One wonders if, as he swallowed, he recalled his words, 'Tak' anither drink, hinny.' Certainly his contemporaries believed that he was reaping the harvest of his brutal deeds.[1]

In this life sin carries its own in-built penalty; it may be physical, psychological or both. God's hand is even now laid in judgment on individuals and nations. When Jacob sinfully deceived his blind father, he suffered exile for many years and later was himself deceived when he wanted to marry Laban's daughter Rachel (*Gen.* 29:21–

[1] This sombre incident is recorded in Alexander Smellie, *Men of the Covenant* (London: Banner of Truth, 1960), pp. 416–20.

25). David's sin against Uriah, involving both adultery and murder, marked a steep downturn in the king's peace and prosperity. 'The way of the treacherous is hard' (*Prov.* 13:15, NASB).

When the Philistines took possession of the Ark of the Covenant, the 'hand of the LORD was heavy against the people of Ashdod and he terrified and afflicted them with tumours . . .' Then the Philistines confessed 'his hand is hard against us'. The lords of the Philistines decided to return the Ark, because the 'hand of God was very heavy there' (*1 Sam.* 5:6–11; cf. *2 Sam.* 24:16).

When Paul faced Elymas, the magician who opposed what he and Barnabas were doing, he said to him:

> You son of the devil, you enemy of all righteousness, full of deceit and villainy, will you not stop making crooked the straight paths of the Lord? And now, behold, the hand of the Lord is upon you, and you will be blind and unable to see the sun for a time (*Acts* 13:11).

And so it came to pass. The Proconsul, Sergius Paulus, whom Elymas was endeavouring to turn away from the faith, saw what had occurred and believed the gospel.

The Psalmist said: 'Your hand will find out those who hate you' (*Psa.* 21:8). Already God's judgments 'are in all the earth' (*1 Chron.* 16:12; *Psa.* 105:7). When a nation that has known the blessings of the Protestant Reformation, and has experienced mighty workings of God's Spirit in revival, turns its back on God and his law and enacts legislation directly contrary to his will, that nation is ripe for God's punishment. God's judgment can come in various ways. He can use the forces of nature as his instrument of punishment. When Israel crossed the Red Sea, escaping from Pharaoh's army, Moses and the people sang: 'You blew with your wind; the sea covered them; they sank like lead in the mighty waters' (*Exod.* 15:10). The Psalmist spoke of 'fire, and hail, snow and mist, stormy wind fulfilling his word' (*Psa.* 148:8).

God can also use sinister forces as his rod to effect punishment. He did so when the people of Judah persisted in their sinful disobedience, using wicked and godless nations like Assyria and Babylon for that purpose. Assyria he described as 'the rod of my anger' (*Isa.* 10:5), and before his people were taken into captivity in Babylon, the Lord referred to Nebuchadnezzar as 'my servant' (*Jer.* 27:6). We need to pause and ask what kind of rod of judgment God is using today. He is the same as he was in the days of Isaiah and Jeremiah; the Lord is the unchanging God.

Temporal judgments from the 'hand of God' are but foretastes of an infinitely greater judgment that shall come at the end of time. God may seem to be silent now and his judgments may not be recognized for what they are, but every judgment that God brings upon nations and individuals in time is an unmistakable warning of the coming cataclysmic judgment, when God will speak for the last time in history.

In Scripture we frequently read of 'the day of the Lord'. It is usually associated with a coming judgement, either upon Israel in time or upon the world at the end of time. Obadiah describes the doom of Edom as 'the day of the

Lord' (*Obad.* 15–16). Sometimes we find predictions of judgment in the not-too-distant future interspersed with clear references to a final judgment. Isaiah having spoken of 'the day of the Lord' when Babylon would be overthrown (*Isa.* 13:6–8), is guided to speak of another day of judgment:

> Behold, the day of the Lord comes, cruel with wrath and fierce anger, to make the land a desolation and to destroy sinners from it . . . I will punish the world for its evil, and the wicked for their iniquity; I will put an end to the pomp of the arrogant, and lay low the pompous pride of the ruthless (*Isa.* 13:9, 11).

Zephaniah, in a similar solemn passage, sees 'the day of the Lord' as a day of wrath, the *dies irae* of classical literature.

> The great day of the Lord is near and hastening fast . . .
> A day of wrath is that day, a day of distress and anguish,
> a day of ruin and devastation, a day of darkness and
> gloom . . . (*Zeph.* 1:14–15).

That is how the day of the Lord will affect the unbelieving, godless, and wicked of this world. What a tragedy that so many have turned a blind eye to the awful prospect that awaits them!

The apostle Paul has much to say of this last day. Sometimes he just refers to it as 'that day' (*1 Thess.* 5:4), or as 'the day'. He also speaks of 'the day of the Lord' (*1 Thess.* 5:2; *2 Thess.* 2:2; *1 Cor.* 5:5), 'the day of Christ Jesus' (*Phil.* 1:6) and 'the day of Christ' (*Phil.* 2:16). Herman

Ridderbos suggests that 'by "the Lord" . . . Christ must be understood', because Paul associates the term with Christ's second coming.[2] That coming day now demands our careful attention for it has everlasting consequences for every single human being without exception.

A DAY OF SEPARATION

In Matthew chapter 25 we have our Lord's description of what will take place on the day of judgment. He will sit on 'his glorious throne'. All nations shall be gathered before him (*Matt.* 25:32). Christ is speaking here of the judgment of the whole human race. The wicked and the righteous will stand before the One to whom the Father has entrusted all judgement (*John* 5:22). At present it is not possible to distinguish infallibly between those who truly know the Lord and those who do not, those referred to as 'the sheep' and 'the goats' in our Lord's parable. At that Grand Assize with Christ as the Judge, the distinction will be sharp and clear. 'No creature is hidden from his sight, but all are naked and exposed to the eyes of him to whom we must give account' (*Heb.* 4:13).

Christ said that on that day 'he will separate people one from another [note that it is individuals, not nations, classes or families] as a shepherd separates the sheep from the goats' (*Matt.* 25:32). Sheep were valued more highly than goats, although it was customary for them to graze together. The shepherd would not fail to distinguish the one from the other. So on the last day, Christ will separate unbelievers and believers, infallibly and permanently. 'He

---

[2] Herman Ridderbos, *Paul*, p. 530.

will place the sheep on his right (the favoured side), but the goats on the left' (*Matt.* 25:33). To those on his right he will say: 'Come, you who are blessed by my Father, inherit the kingdom prepared for you from the foundation of the world' (*Matt.* 25:34). But to those on his left he will say: 'Depart from me, you cursed, into the eternal fire prepared for the devil and his angels' (*Matt.* 25:41). Believers go to a place specially prepared for them (cf. *John* 14:2–3), but unbelievers go to a place prepared for the devil and the demons. William Hendriksen reminds us that not only did our Lord at this time speak of *separation*, but also of *association*, 'the most gruesome togetherness of all'.[3]

Believers are lovingly and tenderly invited to 'Come' and receive their inheritance; but unbelievers are sternly dismissed from Christ's presence with the chilling words, 'Depart from me.' The 'eternal fire' mentioned by Christ is hell. He had just said of hell: 'In that place there will be weeping and gnashing of teeth' (*Matt.* 25:30), anguish and angry frustration. The expression 'gnashing of teeth' in Scripture is associated with anger (*Job* 16:9; *Psa.* 37:12; *Psa.* 112:10; *Lam.* 2:16). Hell is a place of unspeakable and endless torment. Of those who are there, it is said that 'the smoke of their torment goes up for ever and ever, and they have no rest, day or night. . . ' (*Rev.* 14:11).

In certain evangelical circles there is sometimes found a somewhat simplistic view of hell, as if it were like a

---

[3] William Hendriksen, *The Gospel of Matthew* (Edinburgh: Banner of Truth Trust, 1974), p. 890.

seething cauldron into which the godless are tossed indiscriminately. That is a caricature of the truth. There are degrees of punishment in hell. Our Lord told the people of Chorazin and Bethsaida that it would be 'more bearable on the day of judgment for Tyre and Sidon' than for them. He said the same of Capernaum (*Matt.* 11:21–24). On the last day some would receive 'a severe beating', others 'a light beating' (*Luke* 12:47–48). According to Jesus, those 'who devour widows' houses and for a pretence make long prayers . . . receive the greater condemnation' (*Luke* 20:47). The punishment is commensurate with the privileges enjoyed. The Bible makes it clear that all have sufficient evidence of the glory and goodness of God to render them without excuse (*Rom.* 1:20), but some are clearly more inexcusable than others. The punishments are not equal in intensity, but they are equal in extension: in terms of duration the punishment is eternal. 'Shall not the Judge of all the earth do what is just?' (*Gen.* 18:25). Sometimes, after an earthly court case, the accused will say, 'I did not receive justice.' No one will say that when we all stand before the judgment seat of Christ.

Nothing, however, lessens the horror of hell. When the atomic bomb, named 'Little Boy', was dropped on Hiroshima on 6 August 1945, we are told that in the first billionth of a second, the temperature at the epicentre reached 60 million degrees and a 1,000 mph wind spread the heat across the city in a blinding flash of light, facts that stagger human comprehension. The co-pilot of the *Enola Gay* wrote these words in the plane's log book:

'My God, what have we done?'; the tail gunner later admitted that the explosion gave us 'a peep into hell'.[4] When the hydrogen bomb was first tested, it was one thousand times more powerful than the bomb dropped on Hiroshima. The ethics of atomic warfare is not a subject that falls within the scope of this book: the debate continues elsewhere. I simply refer to this petrifying event in human history because I believe it was mistakenly seen as 'a peep into hell'.

Before the bomb was dropped on Hiroshima, several factors had to be, and doubtless were, carefully considered. Sometimes people describe a frightening experience as 'hell'; but no earthly experience, however terrifying, should be given this name. The divine judgment on rampant evil at the time of the Flood and at the destruction of Sodom and Gomorrah was devastating; but although these were expressions of God's anger and judgment on moral corruption that prefigure the final judgment, they must not be termed 'hell'. Hell is the ultimate and incomparable horror and is of a wholly different order from any other earthly catastrophe. It is an everlasting punishment for sin. Its supreme moral dimension reflects the perfect holiness and inflexible righteousness of God. Hell is just as much God's hell as heaven is God's heaven. The pervading evil of this fallen world cries out for a day of judgment. Men and women may, at times, slip through the net of man's justice, which is of course imperfect; but

---

[4] Information and official sources provided in Stephen Walker, *Shockwave: The Countdown to Hiroshima*, (London: John Murray, 2005) pp. 255, 261, 262.

no one will evade the justice of God. That moment of blinding horror at Hiroshima was not 'a peep into hell', but rather a time for man to pause and take stock of this sinful world, over which now hangs the Damocles' sword of this fearsome weapon. However, even the nuclear threat is not beyond the control of the sovereign Lord of the universe, who governs history and sovereignly guides it to his predetermined end, the final judgment and the inauguration of 'new heavens and a new earth in which righteousness dwells' (2 *Pet.* 3:13). For God's people that truth provides great comfort.

We have noted a two-fold separation: between believers and unbelievers, and between unbelievers and God.

The question is sometimes asked: 'How can the wicked be sent away from God's presence, since God is everywhere at the same time (omnipresent)? God's presence, however, is not always coupled with a display of his love, mercy, and grace. In hell God's presence is seen in the burning fire of his anger against sin. In describing hell, the Bible uses symbolic terms like 'fire', 'smoke', 'worm'; but the reality of these terms is infinitely more terrible than human language can convey. It is clear from Matthew 25:46, that as the blessing of the redeemed (25:34) is eternal, so the curse (25:41) of the godless is eternal. Hell is forever.

The same adjective is applied to both the punishment and the reward. Jesus is not speaking of some small experience that would be but for a moment, but of that which has no end. He leaves his hearers in no doubt as to the solemnity of what he is saying. Eternal issues are

The Hand That Judges

involved, and this is so for both those on his right hand and on his left.[5]

Those who deny the doctrine of eternal punishment, whatever their motive, flatly contradict the Lord Jesus Christ. His words allow of only one meaning.

A DAY OF VINDICATION

Because the destiny of each person is fixed at death, some going to heaven and some to hell, it has been said that a day of final judgment is unnecessary, except, perhaps, for those who will still be alive when Christ returns. However, God's Word teaches us that God has determined the final destiny of each person from eternity (*Eph.* 1:4; cf. *Jude* 4). What then will be the purpose of a final day of judgment? The chief purpose of that day will be the revelation of the sovereignty and glory of God to all creation, angels, and men. His glory will be seen both in the gracious justification of his people and in the just condemnation of the wicked on that day.

The Christ, despised and rejected by sinful man, will be seen in his majesty and power. He came to this world to humbly suffer and die for his own. He was the butt of the depraved humour of the wicked: 'I am the talk of those who sit in the gate, and the drunkards make songs about me' (*Psa.* 69:12). How dramatic the change will appear when the 'King of glory' descends from heaven 'with his mighty angels in flaming fire, inflicting vengeance on those who do not obey the gospel . . . They will suffer the

[5] Leon Morris, *Matthew*, p. 641.

punishment of eternal destruction, away from the presence of the Lord and from the glory of his might.' Then the Lord Jesus will be 'glorified in his saints and . . . marvelled at among all who have believed' (2 *Thess.* 1:7–10). It will be the day of Christ's public vindication.

Those who bore the reproach of this world for Christ's sake, often suffering persecution and sometimes martyrdom, will also be vindicated in the judgement. They will be associated with their Lord in the exercise of judgment.

> They will be manifested in their belonging to him, and no one will be able to bring any charge against them (*Rom.* 8:33). They will be placed at his side and with him judge the world, and even angels (*1 Cor.* 6:2–3).[6]

That will be a day of honour and glory for the Lord's people.

> The flaming fire shall not come near them. The voice of the Archangel and the trump of God shall proclaim no terror to their ears. Sleeping or waking . . . or standing at the post of daily duty, believers shall be secure and unmoved. They shall lift up their heads with joy when they see redemption drawing nigh.[7]

It is important to see that there is a radical difference between the judgment found in earthly courts and the judgment of the last day. E. A. Litton writes:

---

[6] Herman Ridderbos, *Paul*, p. 556.

[7] J. C. Ryle, *Practical Religion* (Edinburgh: Banner of Truth, 1998), p. 457.

The analogy of human tribunals must not be applied too literally . . . The ordinary notion we form of these is that, whereas before the trial commences the guilt or inno-cence of the accused party is a matter of doubt, now the case is judicially investigated, evidence produced, and, after the verdict of the jury, sentence pronounced. A human trial, therefore, is strictly a process of *investig-ation*. But we cannot ascribe this character to the so-called judgment of the quick and dead. The Judge is omniscient, and has no need of evidence to convince Him; He presides with perfect knowledge of the charac-ter and history of every one who stands before Him; He has already Himself pronounced a judgment from which there is no appeal, and respecting which there can be no mistake.[8]

Litton states that the last great day will be one of *pub-lication* and *execution*, Christ being perfectly acquainted with the lives of the parties concerned.

On that day when Christ and his people will be vin-dicated, all scepticism will be banished, all rebellion crushed, and all unbelief confounded. Everyone will know the truth, but not everyone will know it savingly. Through the prophet Isaiah, God said: 'By myself I have sworn; from my mouth has gone out in righteousness a word that shall not return: "To me every knee shall bow, every tongue shall swear. . . "' (*Isa.* 45:23). To kneel and to swear implies full recognition of the sovereignty of the One to whom such homage is paid. Paul, referring to this,

[8] E. A. Litton, *Dogmatic Theology*, p. 592

adds the words: 'and every tongue confess that Jesus Christ is Lord, to the glory of God the Father' (*Phil.* 2:10, cf. *Rom.*14:11). This does not indicate the prospect of universal salvation, but that all will acknowledge the Lordship of Christ, some voluntarily and joyfully, others involuntarily, yet submissively.

A DAY OF EXPOSURE

When the Lord comes, he 'will bring to light the things now hidden in darkness and will disclose the purposes of the heart' (*1 Cor.* 4:5). He will illumine the darkness and reveal hidden thoughts, motives, and actions.

To the all-knowing One nothing is hidden; the judgment of the last day will be characterized by openness. No one and nothing will be able to hide in the dark. Elsewhere, Paul speaks of 'that day when, according to my gospel, God judges the secrets of men by Christ Jesus' (*Rom.* 2:16). In that passage, Paul's focus is on unbelieving Jews. Their religion was one of externalism, but God searches 'the thoughts and intents of the heart' (*Heb.* 4:13). Nothing is hidden from him and on the day of judgment nothing will be concealed.

The unseen, the covert, the disguised, the occult, the latent, the ulterior, the enigmatic and the mysterious will all be made plain. The nods and winks, the stealthy and the sly, the secret pass-words, postures, and practices of oath-bound societies will be made manifest before all. No clandestine programme, no cloak-and-dagger organization, no back-door, under-the-counter dealings, no camouflaged immorality, will evade the clear, penetrating light of that great day: all will see; all will know; all will be revealed. Justice will be seen to be done.

Then the false religions will be shown to be idolatrous and corrupt. The pseudo-philosophical systems, ancient and modern, will be exposed as delusions. The compromising subtleties of much modern theology will be condemned. The intrigue and, yes, the *lies* of some politicians will be laid bare and the unrighteousness that dominates this godless world-order will be uncovered and seen as reprehensible. 'But as for the cowardly, the faithless, the detestable, as for murderers, the sexually immoral, sorcerers, idolaters, and all liars, their portion will be in the lake that burns with fire and sulphur . . . ' (*Rev.* 21:8). Chilling language, but such warnings of future judgment are given so that in this life none need despair.

There is no justification for anyone to conclude that because he has told lies or practised idolatry or engaged in carnal lusts or even committed murder he has shut himself off from the grace of God's forgiveness and redemption. It is sinners of every kind that Christ came to redeem (*Mark* 10:45; *1 Tim.* 1:15) and the blood of the incarnate Son cleanses from all sin (*1 John* 1:7).[9]

Writing to the Corinthian believers, Paul reminded them of their previous sinful lives, cataloguing a whole range of evil practices, but then added these wonderful gospel words: 'But you were washed, you were sanctified, you were justified in the name of the Lord Jesus Christ and by the Spirit of our God' (*1 Cor.* 6:11).

---

[9] Philip E. Hughes, *The Book of Revelation* (Grand Rapids: William B. Eerdmans, 1990), p. 226.

Your life, however, may be decent, respectable even religious. But do not trust in such externals. Christ in his teaching revealed the inwardness of sin, and he will expose your secret sins in all their true colours. On that day the evil that seeks to hide itself in the human heart will be brought into the full light of God's blazing holiness, righteousness and truth. Lift a large stone that has not been moved for some time and scores of tiny creatures will be seen scurrying in all directions seeking a fresh hiding-place.

On that day, *the day*, there will be no place for the furtive servants of the evil one to run away and hide. The exposure of evil and its consequences will be full, complete, and exhaustive. If meat is not properly stored it can become infested with maggots, a truly revolting sight! On the day of judgment, this fallen world will be seen to be infiltrated by what is vile: the impure, the corrupt, the vicious, the cruel and the unjust: a sickening scene of depravity, as witnessed daily in the news reports, and fit only for the flames of God's wrath. That day approaches when God will both expose and eradicate everything sinful that pollutes his creation.

I write these words in love and with a sincere concern for your soul. What would you do if you saw a young child carelessly playing near the edge of a cliff, or if you saw someone in trouble in the sea or a house on fire? Without hesitating you would raise the alarm. That is both the right and proper thing to do. I am raising the alarm! 'Awake, O sleeper, and arise from the dead, and Christ will shine on you' (*Eph.* 5:14).

A DAY OF REJOICING

How can we speak of the judgment day as one of rejoicing, when the Bible graphically describes it in terms of darkness, wrath, fire, and calls it 'the great and awesome day of the LORD' (*Mal.* 4:5)? Yet the Scriptures also portray this day as a time of rejoicing. Psalm 98 depicts creation vibrant with joy at the prospect of a day of righteous judgment. 'Let the rivers clap their hands; let the hills sing for joy together before the LORD, for he comes to judge the earth. He will judge the world with righteousness, and the peoples with equity' (*Psa.* 98:8, 9).

Concerning the fall of ancient Babylon, we read: 'Then the heavens and the earth, and all that is in them, shall sing for joy over Babylon, for the destroyers shall come against them out of the north, declares the LORD' (*Jer.* 51:48). At the time of this prophecy, Babylon 'was in the noontide of her glory; and her natural situation was such as might seem to betoken a perpetual continuance of prosperity.'[10] It must have seemed beyond the realms of possibility to speak of the ruin of such a 'superpower'. Babylon, the Babel of Genesis 11, became the symbol of worldly power and pride. Thus boasted Nebuchadnezzar her greatest king: 'Is not this great Babylon, which I have built by my mighty power as a royal residence and for the glory of my majesty?' (*Dan.* 4:30). But Babylon fell to the Persian conqueror, Cyrus, in 539 BC. The symbolism of Babylon's destruction emerges repeatedly in the book of

[10] Patrick Fairbairn, *Interpretation of Prophecy*, (Edinburgh: T. &T. Clark, 1865), p. 212.

Revelation, where Babylon clearly depicts human arrogance and defiance of the authority of God. On the last day this godless city will be crushed and its destruction will be a time of rejoicing. Concerning its overthrow we read in Revelation 18:20: 'Rejoice over her, O heaven, and you saints and apostles and prophets, for God has given judgment for you against her!' (cf. *Rev.* 19:1–2). God is to be praised for his judgments as well as for his salvation. Indeed without the judgment that fell on Christ the Sin-Bearer at Calvary there would be no salvation at all!

On the day of judgment there will be abundant cause for rejoicing. To see our dear Lord, who on earth was crowned with thorns, 'crowned with glory and honour' (*Heb.* 2:9), and executing universal judgment, will be a reason for great joy and exultation. To know that this Judge is also our blessed Redeemer, that our redemption is complete, and that we are vindicated as his people before the forces of darkness that in this world persecuted Christ's saints, will also be great cause to praise God. We shall have our bodies glorified. We shall be gathered together for the first time with the whole multitude of the redeemed, and, above all, forever in the presence of our Prince and Saviour. What a glorious day that will be! To witness with our own eyes the doom of Satan and the righteous punishment of the impenitent and unbelieving, will lead us to glorify God afresh. There can be no sympathy for Satan and his followers on that day; even a modicum of sympathy for God's implacable enemies would be sinful.

The Bible envelops all human experience and world history within the moral judgment of God. We have seen that God executes judgment within history and climactically at the close of history. The apostle Peter spoke of a time when scoffers would say of Christ, 'Where is the promise of his coming? For ever since the fathers fell asleep, all things are continuing as they were from the beginning of creation' (2 *Pet.* 3:4). However, he goes on to say: 'But the day of the Lord will come as a thief' (*1 Pet.* 3:10), suddenly, unexpectedly. That day is 'drawing near' (*Heb.* 10:25). According to God's timetable the Son of Man 'is near, at the very gates' (*Matt.* 24:33). Even now, 'the Judge is standing at the door' (*James* 5:9).

Although the Scriptures focus on God's love and grace, they contain many warnings against indifference to that love and vividly portray the terrors of divine punishment of impenitent sinners. The Saviour was not lacking in compassion when he spoke more often about the woes of hell than the joys of heaven.

Note well that physical death will mark the end of your opportunities to repent and receive forgiveness. 'It is appointed for man to die once, and after that comes judgement' (*Heb.* 9:27). No second chances after death! This makes the matter of salvation very urgent, since none of us knows what a day may bring forth (cf. *James* 4:14). '*Now* is the day of salvation' (2 *Cor.* 6:2). Satan says, 'WAIT': God says 'NOW IS'.

God is the Deliverer; Satan is the Destroyer. To whom will you listen? Whom will you obey?

EPILOGUE:

COMFORT

In these pages we have considered the comfort of having a sovereign God. The word 'comfort' derives from the Latin words *con* and *fortis* meaning 'with strength' or 'to make strong'. Too often the sovereignty of God has been seen as a harsh and cold doctrine; yet that is not how God's reign is portrayed in Scripture. The Bible depicts God's sovereignty in a manner designed to strengthen our spirits and to reassure us in this evil and broken world: in a word, to 'comfort'.

Behind the bravado of this world's politicians and pop stars, 'men's hearts' are 'failing them for fear' (*Luke* 21:26, KJV). No amount of bluster can disguise the vulnerability of human beings. Christian people, conscious of their God's dominion and providence can say: 'Therefore we will not fear though the earth gives way, though the mountains be moved into the heart of the sea, though its waters roar and foam, though the mountains tremble at its swelling.' The nations may rage, the kingdoms totter, but 'The LORD of hosts is with us; the God of Jacob is our fortress' (*Psa.* 46:2–7). Comfort! Our sovereign Lord cares for his children with all the kindness and generosity of a father and with all the love and tenderness of a mother (*Matt.* 7:11; *Isa.* 66:13).

When these truths are rejected, man becomes time-bound and truth becomes relative and subject to change. Life in this world has no ultimate meaning if we are inhabiting a universe that is merely the result of a random happening such as a 'big bang'. How could one feel at home in such an environment that has no reason for existence, no future direction, and no hope after death?

There is no comfort to be found in placing one's faith in 'blind chance'. Why cling to unreal and illusory notions when God has revealed the truth in his Word and pleads with us in grace? Why grope through the mists of modern philosophies when Christ 'the Light of the world' is shining upon you? 'As I live, declares the Lord GOD, I have no pleasure in the death of he wicked, but that the wicked turn from his way and live . . .' (*Ezek.* 33:11).

To you, in this day of grace, God extends his hand in love and mercy. Grasp that hand and experience the joy of salvation.

APPENDIX A:

THE HISTORICITY OF
THE GENESIS ACCOUNT

It is not uncommon to find liberal theologians rejecting the historicity of the first eleven chapters of the book of Genesis, regarding them as a collection of myths designed to convey certain universal truths. There are two factors at work in such rejection: the Genesis account of creation, when carefully considered, does not harmonize with the theory of evolution; and the doctrines contained in the following chapters of Genesis, particularly Chapter 3, are unacceptable to the liberal mind.

However, the remainder of the Bible regards the account of man's creation and subsequent fall as historical. The creation account itself clearly claims to be factual (*Gen.* 2:4).

The Decalogue speaks of God's resting on the seventh day. The Evangelist Luke traces the genealogy of Jesus back to Adam (*Luke* 3:23–38). Matthew, writing for mainly Jewish readers, begins the genealogy of Jesus with Abraham. Clearly he accepted the historicity of the whole of the Genesis account (*Matt.* 10:15; 24:37). Christ and his apostles unreservedly accepted the historicity of the Genesis record.

If the first eleven chapters of Genesis are rejected, then the whole Bible is undermined and the idea of redemptive history is rendered meaningless.

Some Christians hesitate to say that Genesis is mythical in character, but they are also reluctant to accept the Genesis creation account and the record of the Fall as literal history. They prefer to see these portions of the book of Genesis as poetry, which allows for a variety of interpretations.

However, nothing in the book of Genesis requires such a view: the chapters and verses of Genesis are presented as a straightforward, historical account, not as something that is to be interpreted to suit the fancy of the individual. As the Lutheran commentator, H. C. Leupold, says of the Bible's opening book:

> It goes back beyond the reach of available historical sources and offers not mythical suppositions, not poetical fancies, nor vague suggestions, but a positive record of things as they actually transpired and, at the same time, of matters of infinite moment for all mankind.[1]

[1] H. C. Leupold, *Exposition of Genesis* (Grand Rapids: Baker Book House, 1942), vol. 1, p. 25.

APPENDIX B:

THE BANEFUL INFLUENCE OF EVOLUTIONARY THEORY

The formation of man in the image of God was the crowning act of creation. It is this divine image in man that constitutes what may be termed the 'man-ishness' of man.

Man, as God's deputy, was given 'dominion' over all the creatures of the earth (*Gen.* 1:26). Adam 'gave names to all livestock and to the birds of the heavens, and to every beast of the field' (*Gen.* 2:20). Man was 'crowned with glory and honour'. God 'put all things under his feet' (*Psa.* 8:5–6). Nowhere is man's dignity asserted more clearly and boldly. Although man fell and his glory was tarnished by sin, he was still God's image-bearer, however that image may have been defaced.

It is ironic that the man-centred evolutionary theory, that would take God out of his universe, actually dehumanizes man, for it relates him physically and mentally to the brute beast, and sees him as simply an intelligent animal. The dire consequences of such a view of man are well illustrated by the sad religious experience of Charles Darwin, in many respects the father of evolutionary philosophy.

In his youth Darwin gave intellectual assent to historic Christianity. He seriously considered studying for Holy Orders in the Church of England, but found that he could not accept all the teaching of the Church. At Cambridge University he fell into bad company, but did make a few good friends, including Professor Henslow who combined scientific scholarship with the deepest piety. It was with Henslow that Darwin initially wished to read Divinity.

A turning point came in Darwin's life when he joined the team of scientists on board the *Beagle* as a naturalist. He was still at that time orthodox in his religious beliefs. It was on his return home from that voyage that he studied extensively the scientific data that had come before him and became convinced that species originated according to natural law. He consequently rejected the Genesis account of creation.

With his keen mind, he saw that Genesis was an integral part of the Old Testament and, rejecting the authority of the Old Testament, he gradually rejected the whole of Christianity. In his autobiographical notes, he tells how at about the age of thirty his love for poetry, art and music faded. By the time he reached the age of forty he had rejected Christianity as a delusion.

But did he find peace as a self-confessed agnostic? Far from it! For the rest of his life he was dogged by doubts. He no longer believed in the existence of the soul or in its immortality. And yet the evidence of design in the universe plagued him and tortured his thoughts. Near the end of his life, he wrote: 'But then with me the horrid doubt always arises whether the convictions of man's mind, which has developed from the mind of lower animals, are of any value or at all trustworthy. Would anyone trust in the convictions of a monkey's mind, if there are any convictions in such a mind?'

Again he wrote, 'I am, and shall ever remain in a hopeless muddle.'

These details about Charles Darwin, and much more besides, can be found in an article by B. B. Warfield entitled, 'Charles Darwin's Religious Life: A Sketch in Spiritual Biography.'[1]

Warfield makes the following significant comment: 'By such stages did this great man drift from his early trust into inextinguishable doubt whether such a mind as man's can be trusted in its grand conclusions . . . '[2]

So we repeat our statement at the conclusion of the first chapter:

When we choose to exercise blind faith in a man-made theory, we cannot experience certainty, comfort, or hope.

---

[1] *The Works of Benjamin B. Warfield* (Grand Rapids: Baker Book House, 1981), vol. 9, chapter 19.
[2] Ibid., p. 576.

APPENDIX C:

'THE OPEN VIEW OF GOD'

This view of God distorts and undermines the doctrine of his sovereignty. A leading spokesman for it, Clark Pinnock, defines the 'openness' being advocated thus:

> The all-powerful God delegates power to the creature, making himself vulnerable. In giving us dominion over the earth, God shared power with the creature. The fact of sin in history reveals the adverse effect that disobedience has on God's purpose. God allows the world to be affected by the power of the creature and takes the risks accompanying any genuine relatedness.[1]

Again Pinnock asserts that

> Omnipotence does not mean that nothing can go contrary to God's will (our sins go against it) but that God is able to deal with any circumstance that may arise. The idea that it means total control is an alarming concept and contrary to the Scriptures.[2]

---

[1] Symposium, *The Openness of God* (Downers Grove/Carlisle: Inter-Varsity Press/Paternoster Press, 1994), p. 115.
[2] Ibid., p. 114.

He endorses the view that 'God sets goals for creation and redemption and realizes them *ad hoc* in history. If Plan A fails, God is ready with Plan B.'[3] What happens if Plan B fails? or Plan C? What a hopeless thesis! David McKay states that this view likens God to 'an Infinitely skilful chess player' and 'does not mean that nothing contrary to God's will can take place'.[4] How could we trust in such a God? And what would be the point in praying to him?

If our doctrine of God is unsound, all our other doctrines will also be unsound. Consequently, Pinnock can write of what he terms 'a *post-mortem* encounter with Christ', affirming that 'Scripture does not require us to hold that the window of opportunity is slammed shut at death', and he asserts that at the last day sinners will find salvation available if they are willing to have it.[5]

However we interpret 1 Peter 3:19–20, which Pinnock cites, it definitely does not have the meaning he claims for it. The Bible does not contradict itself. The teaching of this professedly evangelical school is utterly false and pernicious. Not only does it make prophecy impossible, but it also deprives evangelism of a sense of urgency. Worst of all, God is depicted as reacting momentarily to circumstances that he cannot foresee – a far cry from the Bible's doctrine of sovereignty! And so the living God of Scripture becomes a Being of human conjecture, freely

[3] Ibid., p. 113.

[4] *The Bond of Love* (Fearn, Ross-shire: Christian Focus Publications, 2001), p. 62.

[5] Clark Pinnock, *A Wideness in God's Mercy* (Grand Rapids: Zondervan, 1992), pp. 168, 171.

manipulated by philosophical theologians, who are bent on devising a Deity after their own imaginations.

This is not merely a negative criticism. Negativity as such is morally and ethically barren. Alfred Edersheim states this well:

> There is not a more common, nor can there be a more fatal mistake in religion or in religious movements than to put confidence in mere negations, or to expect from them lasting results for good. A negation without a corresponding affirmation – indeed, if it is not the outcome of it – is of no avail for spiritual purposes. We must speak, because we believe; we deny that which is false only because we affirm and cherish the opposite truth.[6]

Our repudiation of the so-called 'open view of God' results from our glad acceptance of the biblical testimony to God's absolute and unqualified sovereignty.

[6] Alfred Edersheim, *Bible History: Old Testament*, p. 844.